BLUES HARMONICA

A COMPREHENSIVE CRASH COURSE AND OVERVIEW
by TOM BALL

D1595562

Original Cover Concept – Laurie Linn Ball
Cover Photos – L, *Little Walter, *Big Walter Horton, Sonny Terry,
Tom Ball, *Sonnyboy Williamson ll
Recorded at Gateway Studios, engineered by Juan Garza
Additional photography - Mark Mosrie,
Layout and Production – Ron Middlebrook
* Brain Smith photos

Special thanks to:
Flying Fish Records for permission to include songs from two Tom Ball and Kenny Sultan CDs
Jim Messina for use of his recording studio,
Kenny Sultan for daring me to write this,
Brain Smith for allowing me access to his photograph archives,
Folk Mote Music for supplies and friendship,
Laurie Linn Ball for encouragement, patience and other virtues,
Also to: Mercer Management, Mary Katherine Aldin, Fred Palmer, Steve Baker,
Amy Van Middlesworth, Andy McKaie, Ron Middlebrook, Shannon Leigh Ward, my family and
friends, and to the anonymous photographer who gave me the shot used on the cover.
And finally to the downtown branch of the Santa Barbara Public Library where I spent countless
hors typing this manuscript on one of their coin-operated rental machines, I guess I sort of forgot to
tell them one of their typewriters was malfunctioning so that it didn't require any money.

ISBN 0-931759-72-2
SAN 683-8022

CONTENTS

Track List Numbers	Page
1. Introduction	
2. Play Often, Play Well, Tuning	
Forword	3
Harp History	4
Types of Harps, Diatonic, Chromatic, others	5
Types and Makes of Diatonics	7
Construction	8
Notes of the Diatonic Harmonica	9
Buying a Harp, Breaking it in	11
How to hold your Harp	12
The Tablature System	13
On Style	14
3. Single Notes	15
A Little Theory – (very little)	16
4. C Scale, Straight Harp	17
Various Ditties ~	
5. Taps	18
6. Oh Susanna	19
7. Silent Night	19
8. Swanee River	20
9. When The Saints Go Marching In	20
10. Bending	24
11. Bending Holes 2, 3, 4, 5, 6, 7	25
12. Bending Blow Holes	26
13. The 12 Bar Blues	27
Back Up Harp	31
14. Licks	32
15. Breathing and Phrasing	35
16. Overblowing	36
Playing With A Guitarist	36
Playing With A Rack	38
17. Riffs and Tricks	38
Other Positions	40
Non-Standard tunings	41
Major 7th (Country Tuning) C Harp	
Minor and Other Tunings	
Playing Along With Records	43
Physics	44
Maintenance and Repairs	45
Electric Blues	49
Amplifiers, Microphones	50
SONGS ~	
18. Indiscretion Stomp	54
19. Your Mind Is In The gutter	56
Early Blues Harp On Record	58
Five Great Blues Harpists	59
Bio – The Evolution Of A Harp blower	62
Appendix A, B and C	66
Pseudonyms of Blues Harmonicists	71

FOREWORD

Why another harmonica book? Aren't there already enough of them on the market?

Well, maybe... in researching this project, naturally I took a look at what existed already and came to a few conclusions: some material was a little outdated, some was slanted toward rock & roll; some concentrated strictly on "straight harp", and some was extraordinarily basic.

On the other hand, a couple of the existing books are excellent, and I will be recommending them highly later in this volume. The intention is not to attempt to render other works obsolete, but rather to come up with a somewhat different approach: a comprehensive crash-course on all aspects of the blues harmonica.

Between the covers of this book I'll attempt to convey to the reader most of what I've learned in 30 years of struggling with this beast we know as the blues harp. The overall tone here will be informal. Woody Guthrie was once asked if he could read music, and his answer was: "Not enough to hurt my playing." In keeping with that fine tradition, there is no standard notation here, only tablature. And since it is the nature of any folk music to be passed down aurally, in this case there is also the accompanying cassette tape.

Please try to avoid taking too literally the note-by-note transcription in this (or any other) harmonica book. Blues harp is an instrument that depends upon improvisation and is much more about "feel" than it is about strict technique. There are very few "mistakes."

In a lot of ways, teaching harmonica is like teaching somebody how to wiggle their ears. In the past I've taught guitar, and if someone is making an E chord wrong you can reach over, grab their hand and place it correctly on the fretboard. With harmonica, you can't really shove your hand down somebody's throat to show them what to do (at least, not on the first date). Still, there are hundreds of tips and tricks to share, and I hope this'll help to set folks out on the right path.

Be prepared to drive your loved ones, families, roommates, neighbors and dogs completely up the wall. But if you start to drive yourself up the wall, just put the damn thing down for awhile, relax, take it easy and remember: it ain't brain surgery.

The first blues harmonica record ever made. Daddy Stovepipe, 1924

3

HARP HISTORY

Much has already been written about the forerunners of the modern harmonica and how today's harp, in principle, relates to the "sheng" and other free-reed Chinese predecessors. While traveling in Laos in 1975, I came upon many musicians playing the "khan", an ancient bamboo instrument also related to today's mouth harp. It wasn't until the 1800s, however, that free-reed instruments surfaced in Europe to the extent that the modern harmonica was developed.

Various source materials differ as to who's to blame: some older books claim Sir Charles Wheatstone had a lot to do with it, or Irishman Richard Pockrich, but more up-to-date research has confirmed that the real father of the harmonica was a 16-year-old kid from Berlin named Freidrich Buschmann. In 1821, young Freidrich stuck 15 pitch pipes together and came up with the first recognizable blow-reed mouth harp.

Still, it fell to another German instrument maker to refine and perfect the design. A Bohemian known only as Richter not only added the draw reeds, but came up with the unique tuning system still employed in all 10-hole diatonic harps. This "contribution" may have been, in effect, even more important than Buschmann's initial "invention". Richter's changes took place in the mid 1820s.

The first commercial manufacturer of the new invention was F.R. Hotz, whose tiny company later merged with M. Hohner. The Hohner company was founded in 1857 in Trossingen, Germany. 24-year-old Mattias Hohner quickly built his reputation, and his firm became what is now one of the largest musical instrument corporations in the world.

From the beginning, the U.S. was an important market for the instrument. Perhaps due to the harmonica's portability and low price, it caught on here virtually overnight.

The widespread appearance of the first harps in the U.S. coincided almost exactly with the onset of the Civil War - thus soldiers from both sides began playing them during the hours away from battle. The soon-to-be-emancipated slave population also adopted the instrument as it's own, as did president Abraham Lincoln. During the famous Lincoln/Douglas debates of 1860, Stephen Douglas arrived with a full brass band, while Lincoln carried only his harmonica. Asked to comment, Lincoln is reputed to have replied: "Stephen Douglas _needs_ a brass band, but the harmonica will do it for me".

With the passage of time, the popularity of the harmonica in America has yet to wane. Early medicine and minstrel shows usually featured a harmonicist. Out west, cowboys played them around camp fires. The Black population in the south virtually redefined the instrument by changing the emphasis from "straight harp" to "cross harp", (differentiations which will be covered in detail later in this book). Frank James, brother of Jesse James, alleged that a harmonica saved his life by deflecting a bullet that would have struck him in the chest.

In more recent years, other harmonica history has been made. Little Walter Jacobs, together with Walter Horton and other Chicago blues artists, changed the sound and role of the harp by amplifying it in the early '50s.

Astronaut Walter Schirra became the first harmonicist in space when, in 1967, he smuggled a Hohner Little Lady aboard the Gemini 7 and played "Jingle Bells" to the world via satellite.

Baseball player Phil Lenz, a utility man with the New York Yankees, became the recipient of the largest fine ever levied for poor harmonica playing when manager Yogi Berra relieved him of $200 for playing "happy music" following a particularly bitter defeat.

No doubt more harmonica history will continue to be written. Even as this goes to press, musician Howard Levy is opening up new dimensions by incorporating a revolutionary technique known as overblowing (also to be discussed within). New companies are emerging, and new design changes and prototypes are surfacing from Hohner. Here in the '90s, the instrument is making inroads into classical, jazz and popular music. It's rightful place within the spectrum of legitimacy seems secure, as film scores, T.V. shows and even commercials are utilizing it's unique potential on an unprecedented level. The future of the harmonica seems bright and assured.

TERMINOLOGY

First things first. For the purposes of this book, there is no difference between the following terms: harp, harmonica, blues harp, mouth harp, mouth organ, French harp and diatonic harp. They all refer here to the plain ol' 10-hole harmonica.

If you're looking to play the chromatic harmonica, or the echo, bass harp or special chord instruments, I'm afraid I can't help you much... those things confuse the hell out of me. Now, on to:

TYPES OF HARPS

DIATONIC

The diatonic harp is the standard 10-hole harmonica that is used by the vast majority of players, both amateur and professional. This is the instrument that I am assuming you are now playing (or will be soon).

The word "diatonic" refers to the diatonic scale - the "do re mi" scale. This is an 8-tone scale without chromatic intervals (no sharps or flats). In other words, the notes you would find on the white keys of the piano.

Diatonic harmonicas come in every key; in order to have a complete set, one would need 12 different harps.

So why bother? Why not just buy a chromatic harp, which, theoretically can be played in every key? Well, the answer lies in the way the harps are tuned and constructed.

The diatonic harp is tuned so that players can achieve a correct chord simply by blowing or drawing virtually anywhere on the instrument. (A "chord" means a combination of 2 or more tones played at the same time.)

Also, more importantly, the diatonic has characteristics that enable a player to drastically bend and/or overblow the reeds. We'll be going into this in more detail a little later, but suffice it to say that if you're interested in playing blues harp, you will need to buy a 10-hole diatonic. No other type of harp will enable you to get that bluesy, gutsy sound.

CHROMATIC

The chromatic is an entirely different animal. It is well suited to jazz and classical music, but in my opinion not particularly well suited to blues.

In reality, a chromatic harp is simply 2 harps tuned a half-step apart and then stacked on top of each other. A slide button, located on the right of the harp, covers up either the top or bottom harp, at the player's option. The result is that all the notes of the chromatic scale are then available to the player.

Most chromatics are "solo tuned", which changes the chord configuration. But the main drawback is that chromatics are fitted with windsaver valves to prevent air loss. These valves inhibit the bendability of the draw notes - the real keystone of blues sound. (For a more thorough explanation, see "Physics".)

Sure, there are exceptions to every rule, and some will take issue with this blanket dismissal. There are recorded examples of Little Walter and George Smith, among others, playing blues on chromatic - but it just ain't the same. Try it... you'll see what I mean.

NOTES OF THE DIATONIC HARMONICA

HARP
KEY

	1	2	3	4	5	6	7	8	9	10
Db BLOW	Db	F	Ab	Db	F	Ab	Db	F	Ab	Db
DRAW	Eb	Ab	C	Eb	Gb	Bb	C	Eb	Gb	Bb

	1	2	3	4	5	6	7	8	9	10
D BLOW	D	F#	A	D	F#	A	D	F#	A	D
DRAW	E	A	C#	E	G	B	C#	E	G	B

	1	2	3	4	5	6	7	8	9	10
Eb BLOW	Eb	G	Bb	Eb	G	Bb	Eb	G	Bb	Eb
DRAW	F	Bb	D	F	Ab	C	D	F	Ab	C

	1	2	3	4	5	6	7	8	9	10
E BLOW	E	G#	B	E	G#	B	E	G#	B	E
DRAW	F#	B	D#	F#	A	C#	D#	F#	A	C#

	1	2	3	4	5	6	7	8	9	10
F BLOW	F	A	C	F	A	C	F	A	C	F
DRAW	G	C	E	G	Bb	D	E	G	Bb	D

	1	2	3	4	5	6	7	8	9	10
F# BLOW	F#	A#	C#	F#	A#	C#	F#	A#	C#	F#
DRAW	G#	C#	F	G#	B	D#	F	G#	B	D#

BUYING A HARP

As discussed earlier, there are several different choices out there. Stick to a 10-hole diatonic and don't bother with toy store stuff - buy your harps at a music store.

A logical choice for a first harp would be either a Marine Band or a Special 20, key of C. Later, you'll want to pick up another one in the key of A. I suggest you shop around before you buy - music stores can differ dramatically as to pricing. Some charge full list, while others can offer substantial discounts.

Unfortunately, it's not possible to test a harp before you buy it. Once we stick our grubby little lips on one, we've bought it, Jack. Ostensibly, this is for reasons of public health. It is possible, however, to "test" the harp with a small bellows-like contraption found in many stores. This essentially worthless exercise is supposed to enable the buyer to hear if the harp is out of tune or has a rattly reed. In practice, though, it's a waste of time since the human face exerts an entirely different pressure of breath than does a bellows.

The reality of the situation is that, like guitars, all harmonicas are slightly out of tune both with themselves and with other harps. This is just an unavoidable fact of life, so if you're one of those folks who's blessed (cursed?) with perfect pitch, you might want to stick to the harpsichord and avoid blues altogether. Better, though, take an aspirin, drain a tall frosty glass and don't worry too much about it. It's the nature of the beast.

BREAKING IT IN

There seems to be a lot of disagreement as to the value of slowly breaking in harps. Some professionals and/or teachers claim that a brand new harp ought to be babied and played very lightly for a few hours before really honking on it. This is supposed to extend the life of the instrument, stretch it out, and make it easier to play.

This all may sound good on paper, but in practice it's pretty meaningless. Some harps are stiffer than others, and no amount of coddling can loosen them up. And as far as life expectancy goes, once metal-fatigue sets in, the thing will go flat whether it's been broken in first or not. I've yet to find any basis, either scientific or practical, for the theory that a harp ought to be slowly broken in. Just buy 'em and dig in. Still, if it makes you feel better...

CONSTRUCTION

The basic design of the diatonic harp has changed little in the last 150 years. A simple instrument, the harp consists of a wooden or plastic "comb" sandwiched between 2 reed plates and 2 cover plates.

Each reed plate contains 10 freely vibrating reeds made of brass. The upper reed plate has the blow reeds, the lower reed plate the draw reeds. The reeds are centered above and below each chamber (or hole). Thus, a total of 20 notes (not including bends and overblows) are available by breathing through the harp.

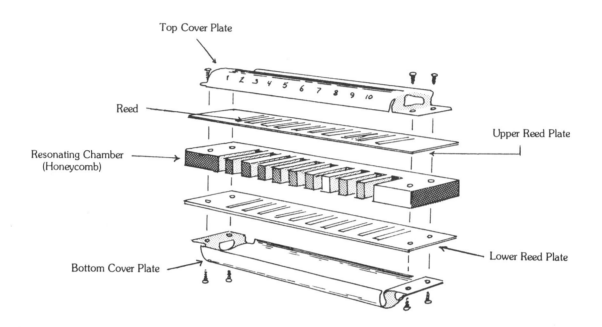

1991 Belgium Rhythm and Blues Festival

8

NOTES OF THE DIATONIC HARMONICA

G

	1	2	3	4	5	6	7	8	9	10
BLOW	G	B	D	G	B	D	G	B	D	G
DRAW	A	D	F#	A	C	E	F#	A	C	E

Ab

	1	2	3	4	5	6	7	8	9	10
BLOW	Ab	C	Eb	Ab	C	Eb	Ab	C	Eb	Ab
DRAW	Bb	Eb	G	Bb	Db	F	G	Bb	Db	F

A

	1	2	3	4	5	6	7	8	9	10
BLOW	A	C#	E	A	C#	E	A	C#	E	A
DRAW	B	E	G#	B	D	F#	G#	B	D	F#

Bb

	1	2	3	4	5	6	7	8	9	10
BLOW	Bb	D	F	Bb	D	F	Bb	D	F	Bb
DRAW	C	F	A	C	Eb	G	A	C	Eb	G

B

	1	2	3	4	5	6	7	8	9	10
BLOW	B	D#	F#	B	D#	F#	B	D#	F#	B
DRAW	C#	F#	A#	C#	E	G#	A#	C#	E	G#

C

	1	2	3	4	5	6	7	8	9	10
BLOW	C	E	G	C	E	G	C	E	G	C
DRAW	D	G	B	D	F	A	B	D	F	A

OTHER TYPES

The <u>Echo</u> is a weird little harp with double holes and 2 reeds tuned to the same note. It sounds kind of like a really sour concertina. For blues, it's virtually unbendable, which means unplayable. In fact, I can't begin to figure out what kind of music this thing is designed for. Does anybody out there actually play one of these things, or is this strictly some kind of remnant from an alpine nightmare?

The <u>Vest</u> <u>Pocket</u> <u>Harp</u> (or <u>Piccolo</u>), is simply a shrunken 10-hole diatonic. Because of it's smaller size, it requires more accuracy and precision to play. One very interesting feature is that the G and A Vest Pockets are tuned exactly one octave higher than their corresponding full-size 10-hole counterparts, which opens up lots of possibilities. (The rest of the Vest Pockets are <u>not</u> tuned higher... <u>only</u> the G and A.) If you play music with a guitarist, a Vest Pocket in A is a very handy supplemental instrument.

There are lots of other harps available - in fact, the possibilities are almost limitless. In the Hohner line alone, there are at least 60 different types, from the 1" long Little Lady to the 384 reed Chord Harmonica. Also the Double Bass Extended, El Centenario, Chordomonica II and Goliath models. But, again, for blues it's best to stick with the 10-hole diatonic.

TYPES AND MAKES OF DIATONICS

There are a lot of different 10-hole diatonics out there... so, which one should you buy? Well, it's really just a matter of personal preference, plus maybe the factors of price and availability. One man's ceiling is another man's floor. My personal choice is the Hohner Special 20, but let's explore a little further. The **Marine Band** is the granddaddy of them all, and the one I learned on. It's the harp of choice for many top players, and is probably the best selling harp in the world.

The comb is made of wood, and the tone is great. The only reason I converted from these to the Special 20 is that the Marine Band's wood sometimes swells to the point where it protrudes from the face of the harp, necessitating a "shave" with a razor blade. Nothing wrong with that; a lot of players simply regard such trimming as routine maintenance. But I'm lazy.

The **Blues Harp** is really a slightly altered Marine Band. It has thinner reeds, and is theoretically a bit easier to bend. Very popular.

The **Special 20** is my favorite - the comb is plastic, so there's never a problem with swollen wood. This is especially beneficial to sloppy droolers like me. Also, the compression is excellent and they're very airtight, which makes them easy to play. Highly recommended.

The **Pro** is sort of a Special 20 in blackface. I'm sure there are some other differences as well, but if so, they're very subtle. It's a great instrument, but I've found that the baked-on black coating comes off if your front teeth bang into the harp enough... and I've got enough bad habits without eating paint chips.

The **Meisterklasse** is the Cadillac of diatonics. Superb construction throughout; a lot of players will settle for nothing less. Personally, I find the contour not as comfortable as that of the Special 20, but that's strictly a matter of taste. Be prepared, though: a set of these will put a major dent in your wallet.

All the above models come from Hohner, but the market has broadened in the last decade, and there are now several other makers with diatonics available.

Lee Oskar has a line of diatonics manufactured by Tombo. These offer a modular construction and are popular with many players. They're a bit fatter in the mouth than the others, and I find them a little trebly for my tastes, but some folks love 'em for just that reason.

Some other companies that have jumped on the bandwagon include Huang, Yamaha, Suzuki, Bandmaster and Hering. In addition, there are lesser priced student models in the Hohner line, like the **Pocket Pal, American Ace, Official Scout,** etc. Probably the best advice is to start out with a Marine Band or Special 20 and experiment for yourself. Avoid all the toy-store junk. Try everything you can afford to, you're bound to find something you'll like. Sonnyboy Williamson II played a bottom-end **Old Standby**!

HOW TO HOLD YOUR HARP

Basically, no set way - what ever's most comfortable for you. Make sure the harmonica is face-up, though, meaning the low notes are on the left. (The little numbers are then visable on the top of the harp.)

How the harp fits into your hands will depend upon how large your hands are. Big beefy paws (like mine) are an advantage. As a general rule, the harp is supported by the left hand, leaving the right hand to pivot, cup, wah-wah and otherwise effect the sound of the thing. (Some lefties might feel more comfortable reversing this.)

A few harpists (including Sonny Terry) play the harp upside-down - i.e. low notes to the right. Obviously in Sonny's case this was no handicap. In The Harp Styles of Sonny Terry, Sonny told Fred Palmer, "They tell me that's wrong, you know. If it is, I don't wanna be right. See, if I hold the bass on the left, and then I start to move on the harp, well, then I ain't got nothin' left down there!" Still, Sonny was the exception rather than the rule.

Below you'll find some photos of various hand placements. Try them all and see what feels most comfortable. My own position most closely resembles the bottom right photo.

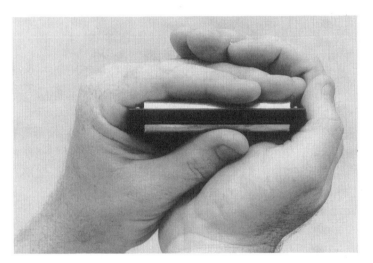
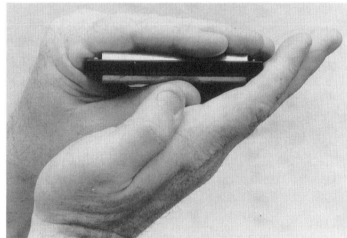

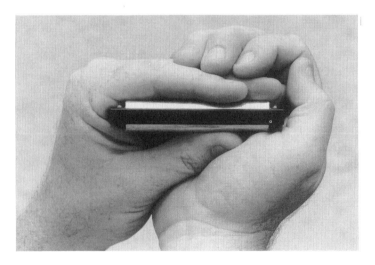
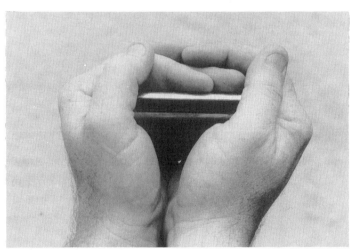

In any case, the object is to form a cup with your hands around the back side of the harp. Experiment with this until this cup is as airtight as possible. The object is not to choke off the sound, but to be able to control it by opening up the cup at strategic times without dropping your harp. The resultant effects will be covered in a few pages.

THE TABULATURE SYSTEM

Harmonica tab really couldn't get much more basic. As you can see by looking at your harp, all the holes have numbers - 1 through 10. In the tab system, those numbers work in conjunction with arrows. An arrow pointing up designates a "blow;" a down arrow is a "draw." Thus, in the example below the player is to blow hole 4, then draw hole 4:

If the arrow is longer, this means to play that note for a longer period of time, as in:

If more than one number is present, the player is to hit all the numbers given, as in:

Obviously harmonica tab is not a complete notation system, but more of a short-hand. The only consideration given as to time is the arrow length, and even that is subject to interpretation. But it's the nature of the harmonica to be freely interpreted, improvised and messed with. If there is any instrument for which standard notation would be too restraining and constricting, it is the harmonica. Later we'll be getting into "bent notes," we at that time we'll be adding a bent arrow to the tab, like this: 4   But don't worry about that for now.

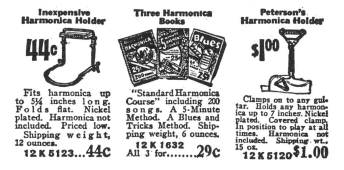

ON STYLE

One night in the mid-'60s when I was about 15, I hitchhiked into L.A. to see one of my guitar heroes, Mr. B.B King. As always he put on a terrific show, after which I hung around the dressing room door, generally getting in the way hoping to get a chance to shake the master's hand. Mr. King saw me standing there, and to my surprise invited me into the dressing room. Ever gracious, if slightly amused, he then introduced me to his band, gave me a hot dog, a few bumper stickers and an autographed postcard. I was in blues heaven! After a time, he asked me if I played music. I remember telling him yes, harmonica and guitar, and that I wanted to play "exactly like B.B." but my hero frowned." Now don't get me wrong," he said, "because I appreciate what you're saying, but you don't wanna play exactly like B.B. King. You see, the world already got one B.B King. What would the world do with two?" Now he was smiling.

"I know you got to go after somebody's style," he went on. "When I was coming up it was T-Bone, and Charlie Christian. But to play exactly like them?" He shook his head. "You see, I had to learn to play like me. You don't wanna copy nobody, man. There's only one you; you got to play like you!"

Best advice I ever got. Thanks, B.

14

SINGLE NOTES

The most important first lesson on the harp is to learn to hit single notes accurately and at will. And it'll take some practice.

The initial tendency is to blow on 2 or 3 holes at the same time. To do so makes a nice chord, and sounds fine - but the essence of blues harp is single notes and bent notes. I cannot overemphasize the importance of accurate single notes.

To start out with, take your 2 index fingers and cover up every hole except 4, then blow into hole 4. That's a single note.

Now take your index fingers away and see if you can repeat this. Chances are your breath is now also leaking into one of the holes next to 4. Without realizing it, you may be hitting 3 and 4 (or 4 and 5.)

Be aware of the shape of your mouth. The opening of your lips must be small - think of yourself as drinking through a straw. Pucker your lips, as though you're saying "oooo," and if you're still having a problem try to alter the shape of the pucker. See if you can make the opening smaller, like a sideways oval.

Some instruction books tout another way to hit single notes: the tongue block method. With tongue blocking, the opening of the lips is larger, encompassing enough space to blow into 4 holes. Then the tongue "blocks out" 3 of them by actually touching the face of the harp, leaving only 1 hole open.

I neither use nor recommend the tongue block method and tend to think of it as a holdover from earlier styles. It is true that by adding and removing the tongue block you can get some unusual rhythm effects which are impossible otherwise - that is, if you want to go around sounding like the calliope at the carousel. Still, each to his own devices. It's just that if the tongue is tied up actually touching the harp everytime you want a single note, then it won't be free to be in the back of your mouth for some other techniques which we'll cover soon.

Sonnyboy Williamson II and friend

A LITTLE THEORY
(VERY LITTLE)

When I first picked up a harp in the early '60s, there were no instruction manuals at all. This was both good and bad; bad because a bit of direction no doubt would've saved me countless hours of trial and error. But good, too, because it forced me to learn by ear which meant I was forced to <u>listen</u>. Frankly, music theory isn't my strong point. Nor, for a harmonica player, does it necessarily need to be. In recent years I've done a lot of studio work (records, commercials, etc.) and I have never seen a situation yet where I was expected to read music. (Basic chord charts, yes, but never actual standard notation.)

Still, at least a rudimentary knowledge of music and of blues progressions is very helpful, even if it's unnecessary to memorize all the terminology. At the time I was learning, if I'd come across a blues harp book full of terms like "mixolydian" or "subdominant," hell, I probably would've chucked my harp in the nearest dumpster and taken up some really challenging instrument like kazoo, or jug (preferably a full one.)

I guess what I'm getting at is that if the theoretical approach turns you off, don't let it scare you away! If need be, you can forget about it for now and come back to it some other time when you want to. But in the meantime, <u>just keep playing!</u> A lot of this stuff you will probably learn by instinct or osmosis, and if such a time occurs that you want to know <u>exactly</u> what it is that you're already doing, then some of that info will be here for you. Having said all that, let's get a bit theoretical.

Death certificate of John Lee Williamson, June 1, 1948

16

STRAIGHT HARP

Playing "straight harp" simply means playing the harmonica in the key for which it was designed - i.e. playing a "C" harmonica in "C." In order to understand the principle, we need to take a look at the way harmonicas are tuned.

All diatonic harps have 10 holes, each of which contain 2 reeds - 1 blow reed and 1 draw reed. The blow reeds are located on the top of the harp, the draw reeds on the bottom. Here's a C harp layout:

DIATONIC C HARP

	1	2	3	4	5	6	7	8	9	10
BLOW	C	E	G	C	E	G	C	E	G	C
DRAW	D	G	B	D	F	A	B	D	F	A

This configuration is known as Richter tuning, named after the Bohemian instrument maker who developed it. Notice the blow notes; they are all either C, E or G. Those of you who have studied a bit of music will recognize that C, E and G make up the 3 notes of the C-chord triad (i.e. the tonic, third and fifth of the C-scale.)

This arrangement is far from accidental. The original premise, no doubt, was to arrange the notes so that no matter where one blows multiple notes on a C harp, a C-chord (in one inversion or another) is the result.

Take a blow on holes 1, 2 and 3 simultaneously. What you're playing is a classic C-chord. Move on up the harp and blow on 4, 5 and 6, and you get the same C-chord one octave higher. Ditto 7, 8 and 9.

Now let's explore the draw notes. They're a little more varied,, and contain G, A, B, D and F. What is the relationship? These notes form a dominant ninth chord (G9) in relation to the root(C.)

Because the harp is set up this way, "straight harp" is particularly suitable for simple melodies, folk songs, campfire ditties, etc. Both the basic melodies and the appropriate chords are readily available. Whenever you hear some cowpoke play "Red River Valley" or "Oh Susanna" in a John Wayne movie, he's playing straight harp.

Is it appropriate for blues? Sure, sometimes - but not all that often. We go into the why and wheres of that in our discussion of "cross harp." But still, <u>straight harp is the place to start</u>! Ya gotta learn to walk before you can run. Straight harp is the easiest way to get familiar with the instrument, and to learn to get around on it. And everything you learn from playing straight harp will come handy later on.

A little earlier we talked about single notes, and the importance of learning to hit just one note at a time. Keep that in mind as you play the following:

$$4 \uparrow \quad 4 \downarrow \quad 5 \uparrow \quad 5 \downarrow \quad 6 \uparrow \quad 6 \downarrow \quad 7 \downarrow \quad 7 \downarrow$$

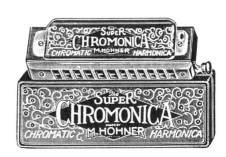

17

This, of course is the C-major scale (do, re, mi, etc.)
Practice this over and over again. Now try it backwards:

If it sounds too full, you're probably hitting more than one note at a time. Make the opening in your mouth smaller and try it again. No tongue blocking allowed!

If something sounds rattly, don't immediately assume you have a defective harp. More likely, you're simply drawing harder than you need to. Try playing it softer.

Sure, I know it's kinda stupid just to play the scale over and over again - but the purpose is to get you used to playing single notes. Once you feel like you've got it, then go on to one of these insipid little tunes:

Here's one everybody knows. It only involves blow notes.

TAPS

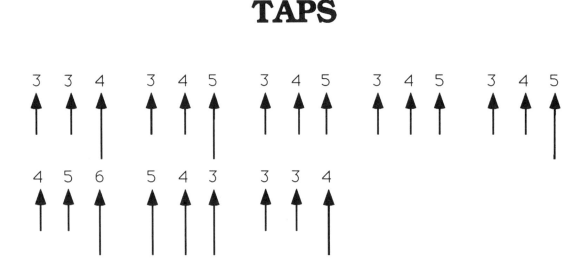

Remember that the longer arrow means to hold that note longer.

Taps is very forgiving, in that if you're having problems hitting single notes it still sounds pretty much OK. This is due to the way the harp is tuned. But, again, the object here is to hit single notes.

Now let's incorporate the draw reeds. I'm assuming you all know how this one's supposed to go:

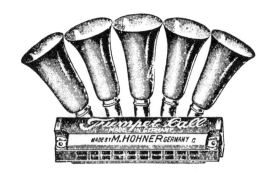

OH SUSANNA

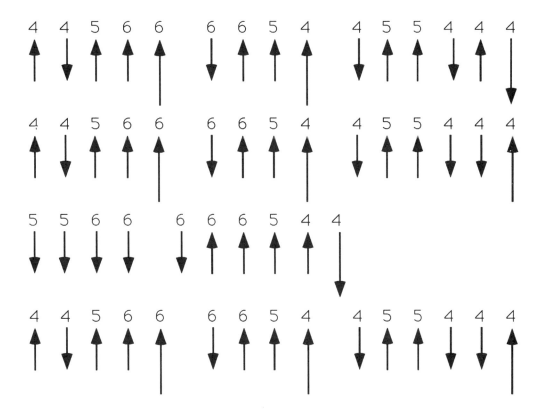

Now, again, straight harp by nature is very forgiving. As long as you've got the wind direction right, this'll sound OK even if you're muffing it and hitting more than one note at a time. But the object is obviously not to muff it, so practice it 'til you're <u>sure</u> you're only hitting one note at a time. (Incidentally, the scale and all of these little ditties are played on the accompanying cassette.) Now here's a few more to try:

SILENT NIGHT

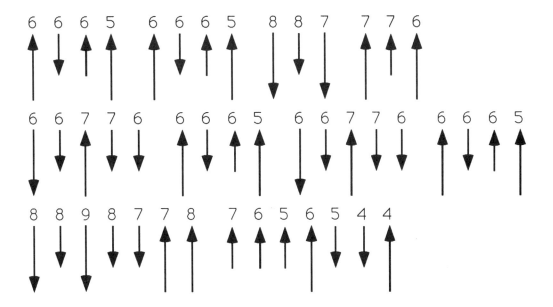

SWANEE RIVER

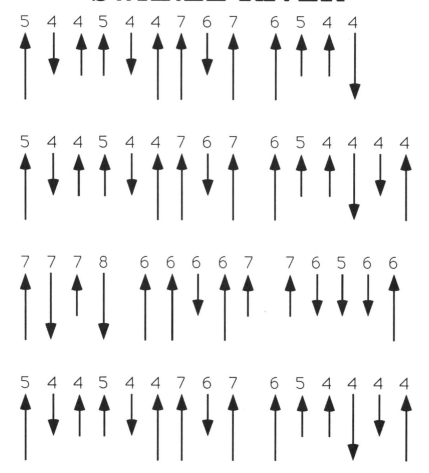

WHEN THE SAINTS GO MARCHING IN

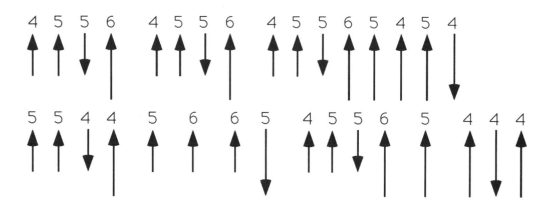

So, you're probably saying to yourself, "Wait a minute, this is supposed to be a blues harmonica book! What's with all this other junk?" Well, the purpose is to familiarize the player with the simple basics of getting around on the instrument, to get the feel of the thing. So bear with me for just a little while more, then we'll move on.

Just about any folk melody, children's tune, T.V. theme or even advertising slogan can be easily figured out and played, straight harp style. Just remember you'll want to use #4 blow as the root note. In workshops I've had scores of students simultaneously blowing such ridiculous stuff as the *Leave It To Beaver* theme song, the Old Spice commercial, the Andy Griffith show, the old Bryllcreme ads ("'A little dab'll do ya"-remember that?) et cetera, ad nauseum. Unfortunately, we live in a litigious society, and I'm not able to put these items in this book because of copyright considerations, but try figuring 'em out on your own - they're easy and fun.

PS - If you lean in close to the mike while playing (like I did on the accompanying cassette tape) you'll wind up sounding like Monica Seles at Wimbledon, because the mike picks up all the little mouth noises and grunts... oh well, that's show biz!

1953 Cad, Tom Ball, Kenny Sultan and Zack. 1981 Photo

CROSS HARP

To understand cross harp is to understand blues harp - it's that basic. The overwhelming majority of all recorded blues harmonica (as well as bluegrass, country and rock n' roll) is played in this position and manner. So what is cross harp?

Cross harp is simply the common name for second position or Mixolydian mode - but don't let that scare you. In essence, all it means is that instead of #4 blow being the root note (as in straight harp,) now #2 draw is the root note.

Somewhere along the line, somebody discovered that if a player were to emphasize the draw notes and bend the draw notes, that a very bluesy sound was the result. And that if the root note was the #2 draw, the ensuing scale would lend itself toward that kind of sound. Hence, cross harp.

So what does it mean to the player? It means that you are no longer playing the harp in the key for which it was designed. In fact, the harp you use is 4 steps up the scale from the key you want to play in; thus, to play in C you'd need an F harp. Take a look at the following chart:

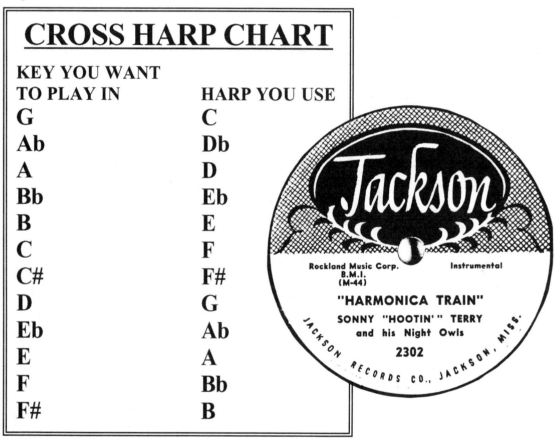

CROSS HARP CHART

KEY YOU WANT TO PLAY IN	HARP YOU USE
G	C
Ab	Db
A	D
Bb	Eb
B	E
C	F
C#	F#
D	G
Eb	Ab
E	A
F	Bb
F#	B

Let's suppose some guitar player says to you: "Hey, let's play in A." Taking a peek at this chart will tip you off that you'll need to grab your D harp.

I often recommend to beginning students that they Xerox this chart and keep it with their harps until they've memorized it. Another idea is to mark each harp case with a magic marker, noting which cross key each plays in. Eventually, though, you'll need to memorize this information.

By playing in cross position, the emphasis of the wind direction will change. In other words, instead of primarily blowing your harp, you will be primarily drawing. Blues harp is at least 80% draw notes, so warm up your chops and get ready to suck!

From here on out in this book (with the exception of a brief discussion entitled "other positions") all of the examples, techniques, exercises and notated solos will be cross harp. This is the position and style to concentrate on.

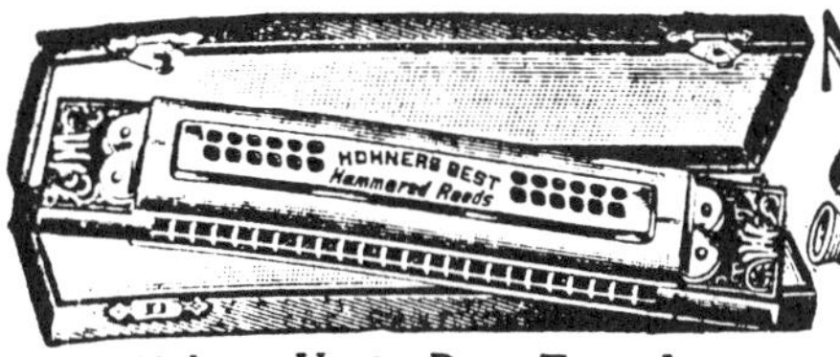

MOUTH ORGANS

MUSICAL PALS

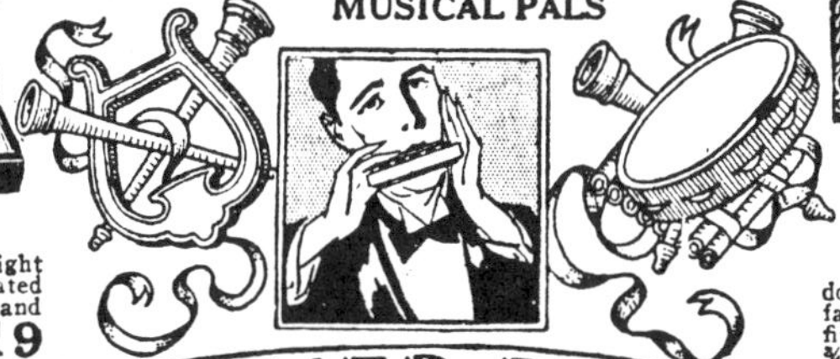

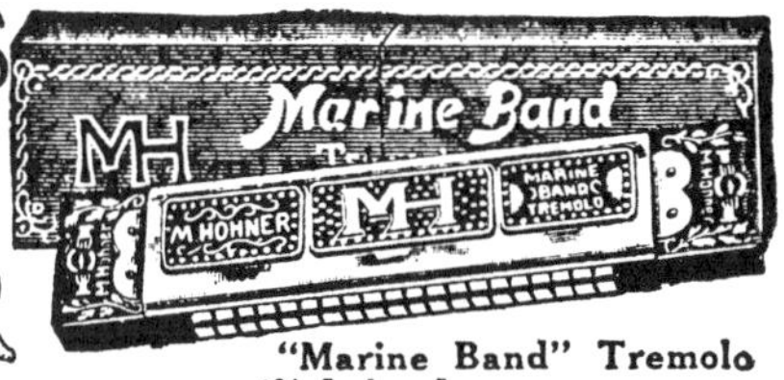

Hohner Up to Date Tremolo

Two harmonicas in one, in different keys. Forty-eight double holes, ninety-six reeds, brass plates, nickel plated covers. Comes in handsome case with metal hinges and clasps. Length, 9 inches. Shipping wt., 1 lb.
12K5144.............................. **$2.19**

"Marine Band" Tremolo
8⅜ Inches Long

A double sided harmonica in two different keys. Forty double holes, eighty tremolo tuned reeds, brass plates, fancy nickel plated covers, nicely ornamented; mahogany finish frame with gilt decorations. Shipping weight, ¾ pound.
12K5141.............................. **$1.49**

HOHNER BRAND

Order Book 12K1645, below, sold only with Harmonicas.

Hohner "Goliath"
7½ Inches Long

A large tremolo harmonica. Twenty-four double holes, forty-eight reeds, brass plates. Case of imitation alligator skin with metal clasp and hinges.
12K5140—Shpg. wt., ¾ lb... **$1.23**

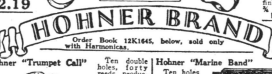

Hohner "Trumpet Call"

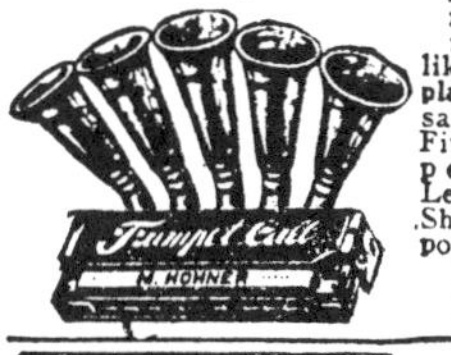

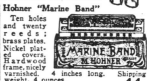

Ten double holes, forty reeds, producing an organ-like tone; brass plates. Has wind saving device. Five brass trumpet horns. Length, 4⅞ in. Shipping wt., 1 pound.
12K5148
$2.19

Hohner "Marine Band"

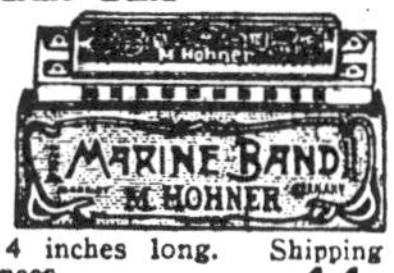

Ten holes and twenty reeds; brass plates. Nickel plated covers. Hardwood frame, nicely varnished. 4 inches long. Shipping weight, 4 ounces.
12K5133.............. **44c**

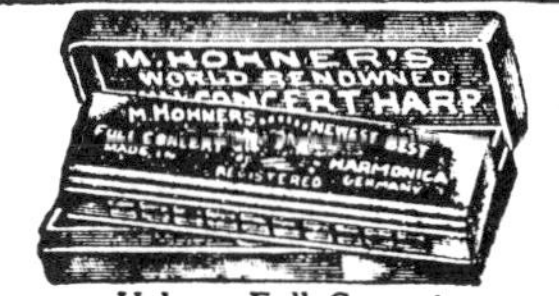

Hohner Full Concert

Ten double holes, forty reeds, brass plates. Covers, finely nickel plated and have overlapping ends. 4⅝ inches long. Shipping weight, 5 ounces.
12K5131.............. **63c**

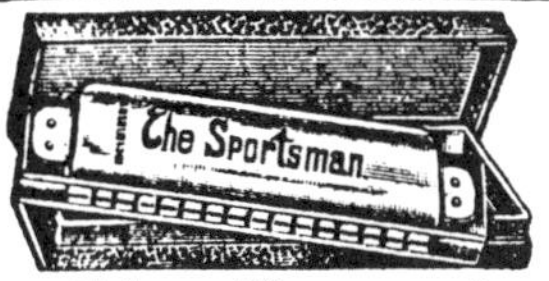

Hohner "Sportsman"

Sixteen double holes, thirty-two tremolo tuned reeds, brass plates, nickel plated covers. 5¼ inches in length. Shipping wt., 6 ounces.
12K5137.............. **59c**

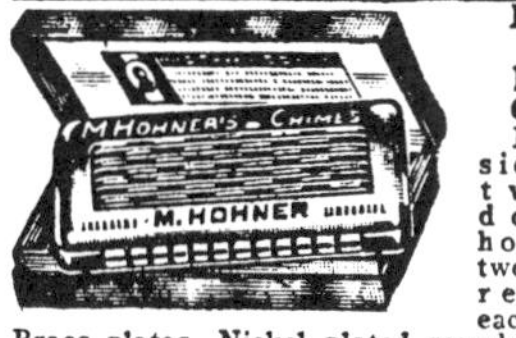

Hohner Vest Pocket Chimes

Double sided with twelve double holes and twenty-four reeds on each side. Brass plates. Nickel plated rounded covers. 4¾ inches long and 2 inches wide. Shipping weight, 7 ounces.
12K5130.............. **83c**

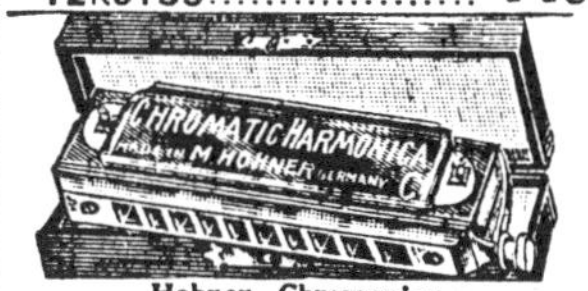

Hohner Chromonica

Twenty holes and forty powerful reeds with wind saving device. Brass plates and heavy nickel plated covers. Mouthpiece is nickel plated, with a slide for producing the half tones. Length, 4¾ inches. Shipping wt., ¾ lb.
12K5150.............. **$2.37**

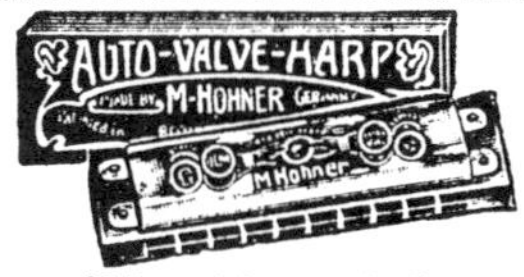

Hohner "Auto Valve"

Has a wind saving arrangement making it as easy blowing as any single reed mouth organ. Ten double holes, forty reeds, brass plates, nickel plated covers; 4⅝ inches long. Shipping weight, 5 ounces.
12K5139.............. **88c**

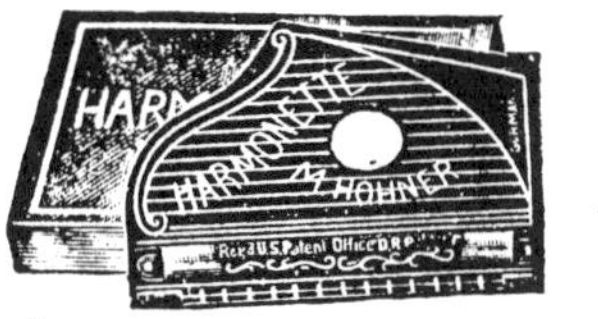

Hohner "Harmonette"

Fourteen double holes, twenty-eight reeds, genuine brass plates and nickel plated covers. Resonator or sound box of wood, reinforced with metal back. A beautiful effect can be produced with it. Length, 4⅝ inches. Shipping wt., ¾ pound.
12K5147..... **83c**

Harmonica Holder

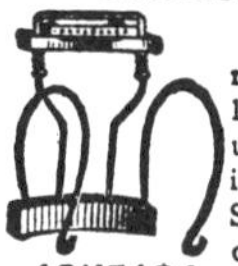

Will fit harmonica not more than 4¾ inches in length. When not in use it may be folded into small compass. Shipping weight, 5 ounces.
12K5124.............. **48c**

Hohner "Echophone"

Finest tone effect can be produced. Horn is 4½ inches long, and made of heavy solid brass. Ten single holes, twenty reeds, brass plates, nickel plated covers. Shpg. wt., 8 oz.
12K5134... **83c**

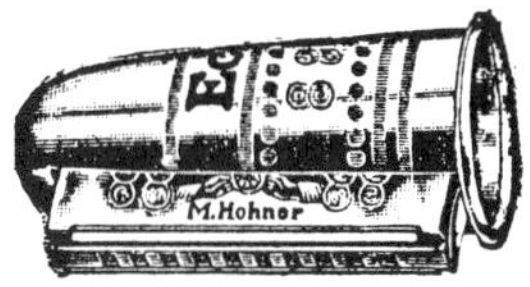

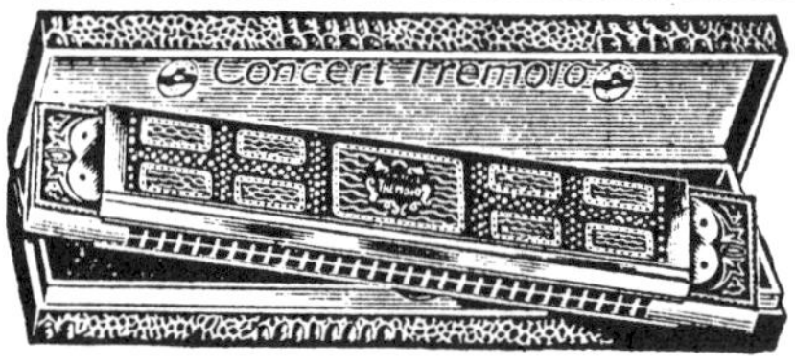

BEAVER BRAND

Order Book 12K1645 with your Harmonicas

Beaver Concert Tremolo

Large double sided harmonica with 30 double holes on each side and 120 tremolo tuned reeds. Heavily nickel plated covers perforated in beautiful design. Hardwood frame with decorated extension ends. 10 inches long. Fancy imitation alligator box. Shipping weight, 1¼ pounds.
12K5125.............................. **$1.65**

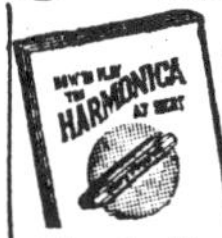

Play the Harmonica at Sight

Shows how to obtain half-tones, trills, tremolos and all kinds of variations. Thirty-two pages. Shipping weight, 2 ounces.
12K1729..23c

Beaver Regimental Band

A favorite with ten holes and twenty reeds. Brass plates. Nickel plated covers. A dandy; 4 in. long. Shpg. wt., 4 oz.
12K5121
21c

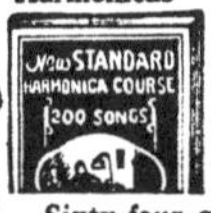

New Standard Harmonica Course 200 Songs

Sixty-four pages with playing instructions and collection of 200 songs such as, "Turkey in the Straw," "Old Black Joe," "When You and I Were Young, Maggie," "Aloha Oe," "Home, Sweet Home," etc. Simple and easy and anybody with little practice can play any song in this book. Shipping weight, 2 ounces.
12K1645—Sold only with mouth organs...... **12c**

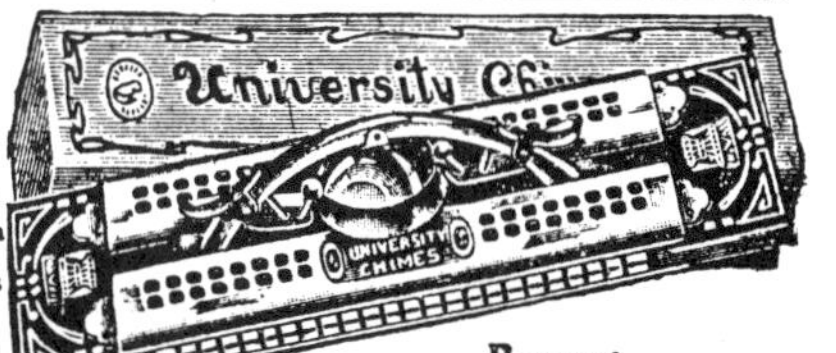

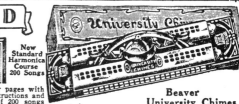

Beaver University Chimes
9¼ Inches Long, Two Bells

Double Harmonica, tuned in two harmonizing keys. Decorated frame, forty-eight holes on each side. Twenty-four reeds on each of four plates or ninety-six reeds in all. Four separate nickel plated covers. Two bells on a special bridge-like frame. Shpg. wt., 1¼ lbs.
12K5118.............. **$1.45**

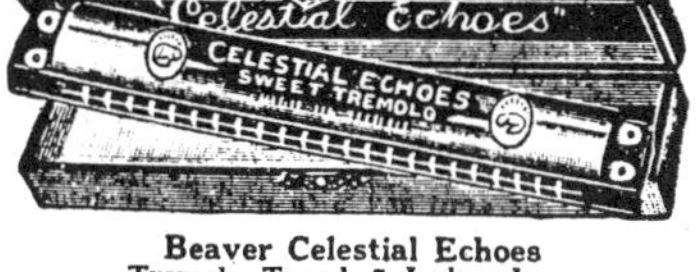

Beaver Celestial Echoes
Tremolo Tuned—7 Inches Long

Brass plates, twenty-four double holes, forty-eight reeds. Handsome paper covered wood box with metal clasp. Sweet, powerful tone. An exceptional value. Shipping weight, ¾ pound.
12K5114.............................. **65c**

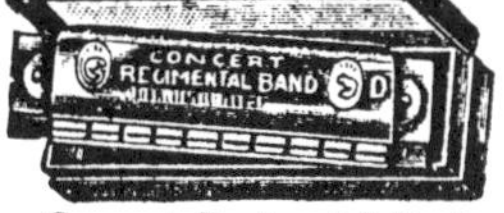

Concert Regimental Band

Brass plates, ten double holes, forty fine reeds. Heavy nickel plated covers. 4¾ inches long. Shpg. wt., 5 oz.
12K5122.............. **43c**

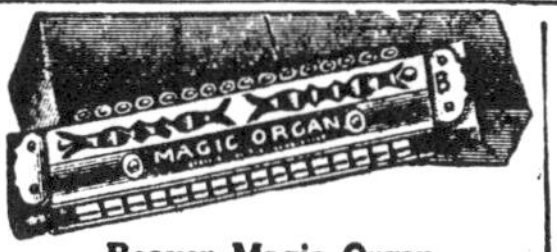

Beaver Magic Organ
Length, 8⅝ Inches

Double covers with imitation organ pipes. Tremolo or wavy effect in tone. Sixteen double holes, thirty-two reeds. Brass plates. Shipping wt., 5 oz.
12K5126.............. **35c**

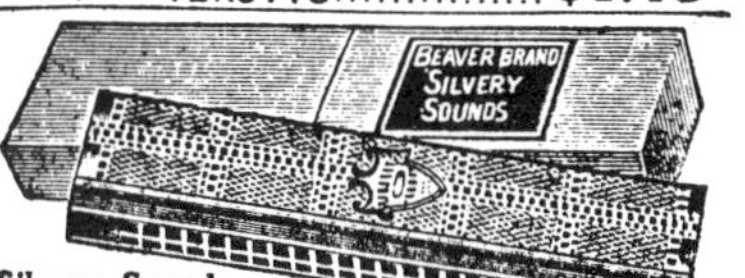

Silvery Sounds
Double Sided
7 Inches Long

Forty-eight holes and forty-eight reeds on each side. Brass plates. Covers are nickel plated and neatly chased and perforated. Tremolo tuned.
12K5116—Shipping wt., ¾ lb......... **95c**

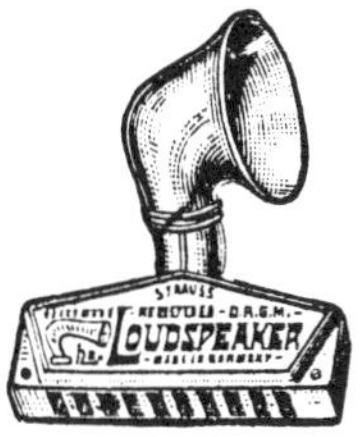

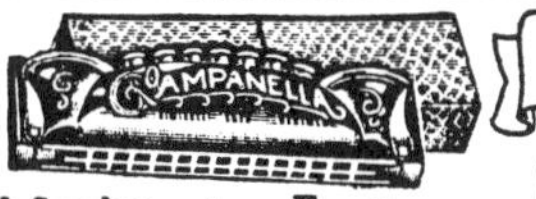

LOWEST PRICES

Send for Book 12K1645 above.

Loud Speaker Harmonica

Brand new. With it even a beginner can easily get the same effects a professional does. Easy blowing, full toned harmonica with a detachable loud speaker horn. The horn is nickel plated with gilt inside bell. Ten holes and 20 reeds. Four inches long. Shipping weight, 1 pound.
12K5154.............................. **42c**

Fourteen Trumpets

Sixteen double holes and thirty-two reeds. Nickel plated covers, fancy design. One of our best sellers. Length, 4¾ inches. Shpg. wt., 5 oz.
12K5152
23c

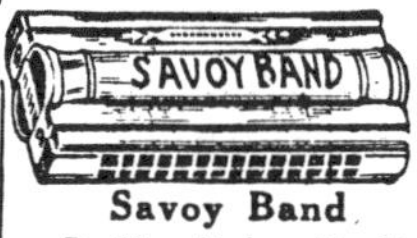

Savoy Band

Double sided, with 14 double holes and 28 reeds on each side. Brass plated plates and nickel plated covers. Mahogany finish frame. Length, 4½ inches long. Shipping weight, ¾ pound.
12K5127..... **39c**

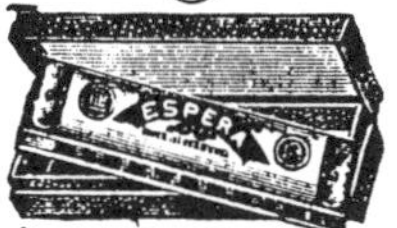

The Espera

Ten holes, twenty reeds, genuine brass plates, nickel plated covers. Priced as low as most with imitation brass plates, 4 in. long. Shpg. wt., 3 oz.
12K5101... **17c**

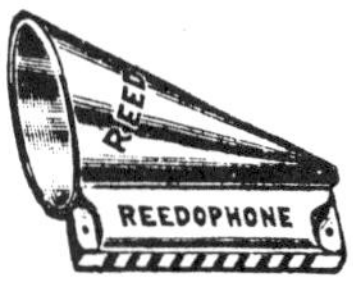

Reed-o-Phone

Ten-hole, twenty-reed harmonica with a horn attachment which is an extension of the covers. Brass plated plates. 4 inches long. Shipping weight, ¾ lb.
12K5128... **33c**

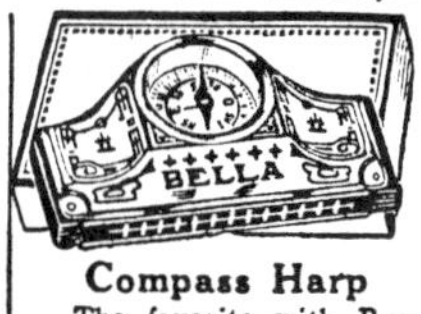

Compass Harp

The favorite with Boy Scouts as it has an accurate compass mounted in the top. 14 double holes and 28 reeds. Hardwood frame, nickel plated covers. Length 4⅝ inches. Rich in tone and easy to blow. Shipping weight, 6 ounces.
12K5153... **65c**

See Index and Information Pages 542 to 570 P **677**

BENDING

WHAT?

"Bending" notes is simply another way to describe the flattening or downward alter-ing of the pitch of a given note. <u>Learning to accurately bend notes is the key to playing blues harmonica.</u>

HOW?

The bend is achieved by altering both the shape of the mouth and the nature of the wind supply. A tone on the harmonica can only be bent <u>downward</u> in pitch; it's impossible to bend a note upward (although it is possible to create the illusion of an upward bend - we'll explore that in a couple of pages.)

WHY?

There are several reasons for bending notes. As we discussed earlier, the diatonic harp is only capable of producing a limited number of tones, and does not include all the notes of the chromatic scale. By learning to bend the existing notes, a player expands the capability of the instrument dramatically. Perhaps even more important, the very nature of the bent note is the essence of blues. If we listen to an expert blues guitarist, for example, we'll constantly hear bent strings - the creation and release of tension employed by this glis-sando effect is a cornerstone of blues.

The basis for bent (or "blue") notes probably comes from the West African vocal scale, which employs minor thirds, flatted fifths and minor sevenths. These effects have be-come so much a part of contemporary music that they are often taken for granted by both vocalists and instrumentalists.

To illustrate just how important bent notes can be, take a listen to the cassette. On it I'll play a simple blues phrase both with and without bent notes - the differences speak for themselves.

CROSS HARP

The main reason that cross harp is the favored position for blues has to do with the bent note. As we shall see, <u>on the lower 6 holes of the harp it is impossible to bend the blow reeds - only the draw reeds can be bent.</u> And since bent notes are the keystone of the blues sound, we will want to employ them often; thus, we must draw often. The result be-comes cross harp. (See chapter on cross harp if confused.)

GETTING STARTED - DRAW BENDS

First of all it's extremely difficult to bend 2 notes at the same time - therefore, if you're still having trouble hitting one note at a time you will not have success bending. Practice is essential... don't jump the gun. Be sure you are comfortable with single notes.

Take an inhale on hole #1. Listen to the note and memorize how it sounds. Now, as you're drawing in air, experiment with changing the pressure and shape of your mouth. Try sucking harder and moving your jaw around slightly. Various people have success with various techniques, so you might try some of the following:

1. Say "oooh - aaah - oooh - aaah" to yourself while drawing the note.
2. Say "oooy - oooy - oooy."
3. Raise and/or lower your jaw a bit.
4. Shift your tongue back in your mouth.
5. Pinch the wind supply by tightening the tension in the throat.
6. Tense your lips slightly.
7. <u>Suck harder</u>!

At least one of these techniques (or perhaps all of them in conjunction) ought to work for you. The result should be that the note dips <u>downward</u> in pitch.

Is it working? If not, keep messing with it - it'll come. Bending can be elusive at first... I recall having a terrible time with it until suddenly it just hit me. Norton Buffalo describes the phenomenon as akin to trying to suck a really thick milk shake through a straw... a big chunk of ice cream'll get stuck, necessitating more pressure, but then it eventually comes free with a thunk. That "thunk" is the bend.

Once you've gotten to the point where you can make #1 draw go down in pitch, move up the harp to #2 draw and try it there. This'll be a little harder because there are now holes both to the left and the right of the hole you're working. Again, make sure you're <u>only</u> hitting #2 draw. Give it a shot. Now try #3 draw, and #4, etc., right on up the harp.

What you'll notice is that once you get way up the harp (#7-#10) it'll get impossible to bend the draw notes. This is due to the harp's construction, not your playing, so don't worry about it.

BENDABILITY

The various holes have differing amounts of "bendability" - that is to say you can bend certain holes further in pitch than others. Hole #2 can be bent 2 semitones, hole #3 can be bent 3 semitones, and holes #1, 4, 5 and 6 can only be bent 1 + semitone. These factors apply no matter what key harp you use, and are the direct result of the Richter tuning.

Bending these draw notes (#1 - #6) is something you will want to practice again and again and again! <u>This is the single most important technique in blues harp!</u>

"UPWARD" BENDS

Again, it is not possible to bend a note upward in pitch; we can only flatten a note downward. But let's look a little closer:

Try bending hole #2 draw. Start out by drawing normally, then slowly bend it down in pitch, and then slowly release the bend until it returns to it's normal pitch. On a graph, such a tone would look like this:

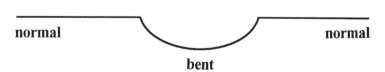

As you've just discovered, if you allow your mouth to return to "normal" while bending a note, the pitch rises back up to "normal." Let's look at that graph again:

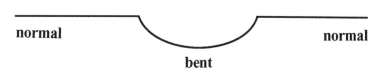

If we chop off the first part of the graph, in other words if we start the note <u>already</u> <u>bent</u> and simply release the bend, then the graph looks like this:

normal

bent

In a nutshell: while we can't truly bend a given note upward, we can create the illusion of an upward bend by pre-bending the note downward, and then simply releasing the bend. Like everything else, this takes practice. You'll need to attack the note in a more aggressive fashion and really bite into it.

The more comfortable you get with pre-bending, the easier everything else becomes. Another technique is to chop off both the first part and the last part of this graph... in other words, to hit only the bent part of the note. To do this adds a (previously unattainable) note to your harp. Extrapolate this over the entire harp and you've now added a lot of new notes.

HIGH-NOTE BLOW-BENDS

These are not as essential to master as the draw bends, but they do add a lot in terms of variety and dynamics.

As we discovered earlier, on the bottom holes of the harp, only the draw notes can be bent. It is a quirk in design, though, that on the top holes, only the blow notes can be bent.

The technique used to get these high-note blow-bends is somewhat different, and a bit more difficult. Right off the bat you'll notice that they are much easier to accomplish on lower-keyed harps, so try this out on a G. A, or Bb harp. (You'll find it nearly impossible on, for example, an F harp.)

First let's isolate #9 blow on an A harp. Play it lightly and listen to the tone. Now, purse your lips, blow harder, and raise your tongue upward as you blow. Hopefully, the result will be a downward lowering of the pitch. Again, this technique is not easy at first - you may have to mess around with it for awhile before it clicks. Keep trying though, and eventually it'll come to you. Incidentally if you're a feline fancier, this'll drive your cats right out of the house... also, this turns some dogs into psychopathic howling banshees, which may open up a whole career for you on Letterman's "Stupid Pet Tricks." Just put my 15% in the mail. These blow-bends are particularly handy on holes #8-#10. Take a listen to Jimmy Reed for a lesson from a master of this technique

---

IN SUM

   Basically, blues harmonica is nothing more than a series of bent, unbent and partially bent notes strung together in cohesive phrases over a skeletal structure. Later on I'll map out (in tablature) many of the most recurrent phrases, together with a bunch of riffs and tricks - but before we go on, <u>practice bending until your lips bleed!</u>

---

12 BAR BLUES

Without getting too much into theory, you should know that 12 bar blues refers to one of the most common structures in music. A "bar" (or measure) is a section of time, and if a song is a 12 bar blues, then each verse is made up of a recurrent pattern of 12 equal time segments. Most blues songs employ only 3 underlying chords. In a 12 bar pattern, these 3 chords change in a predetermined manner. The 3 main chords used in blues are the I, IV and V of the scale, (also known as the tonic, subdominant and dominant.)

So, how does this relate to harp? These chord changes represent the way the underlying structure of a 12 bar blues song will work.

A basic 12 bar blues structure would look like this:

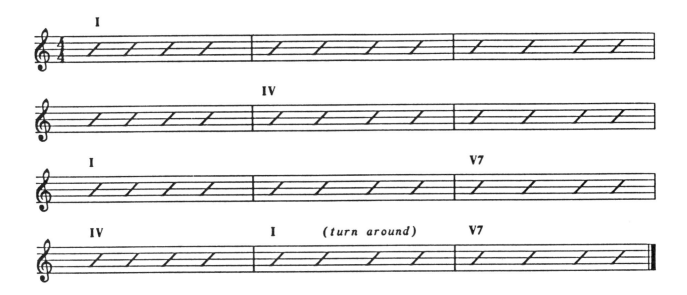

Notice that there are 4 lines, each made up of 3 segments (or bars,) for a total of 12 bars. Also notice that each bar has 4 beats. Now let's translate these changes into harp-ese:

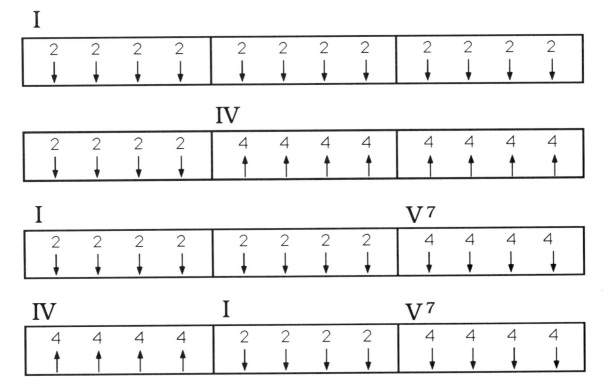

This is the harmonica tab for the most basic way to play along with these underlying chord changes. Try pulling out a harp and playing the above chart, tapping your foot along at every beat. Try it slowly at first, so you'll get the feel for it.

As you can see, there are only 3 chords involved. The purpose of this exercise is to thoroughly familiarize you with <u>where</u> the changes occur... play this over and over 'til you wanna puke or commit suicide.

By now maybe you've figured out that you already <u>knew</u> this stuff, even if you didn't <u>know</u> you knew it. That's because the 12 bar structure is so commonplace in American music that it's probably ingrained in all of us.

If you are familiar with blues (or rock n roll) at all, you probably are aware of countless songs containing verses made up of 3 lines in the following pattern:

I'm going to Kansas City; Kansas City here I come,
I'm going to Kansas City; Kansas City here I come,
They got some crazy little women there, and I'm gonna get me one.

Thousands of blues songs are set up this way; i.e., one line repeated twice, then a third (resolving) line. Let's superimpose these lyrics over our chart:

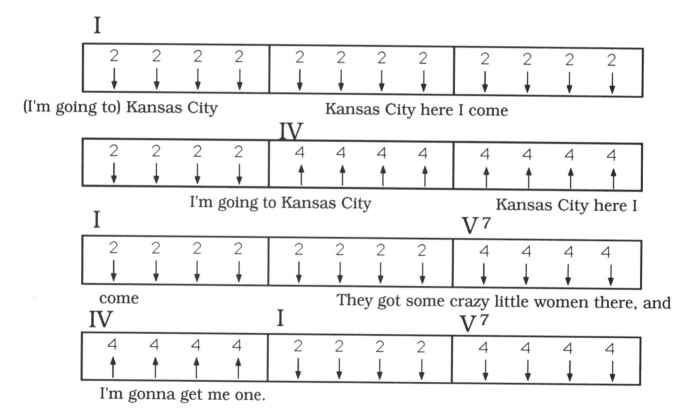

Again, the purpose here is that of familiarization with the chord changes. Once you figure you've got this pattern set in your mind, then feel free to forget about the theoretical side for awhile and let's get on with blowin' some blues! That's right!

28

12 Bar Blues On The CD

The <u>first verse</u> is guitar only, and is merely meant to familiarize you with the structure. If you boost the left channel on your stereo, you'll hear me counting along with the structure.

The <u>second verse</u> features only the very basic harmonica tabbed out a couple of pages ago. It's lightly played, again in the left channel.

On the <u>third verse</u> I lightly play the trills outlined in the next chapter (Backup Harp.)

M-464

How to Play Blues on the **Harmonica**

also Amusing Harmonica Novelty Effects *and* Tricks

A 5-minute Instruction Course

PRICE

ILLUSTRATIONS and easy-to-understand directions make it possible for anyone to perform "blues" and other novelities on the Harmonica in a few minutes.

50c

Old instructional book (courtesy of Scott Dirks)

Here's the tablature to the optional solo I played on the <u>fourth verse</u>: (Some of this is more advanced, so you may have to come back to it after learning some of the riffs and tricks)

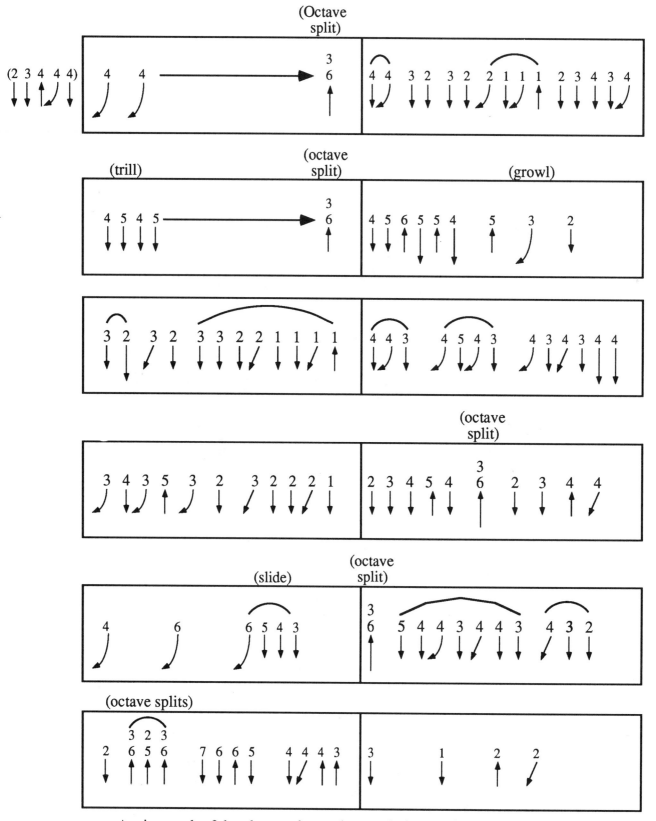

Again, much of the above solo employs techniques which we have yet to cover, so don't panic. When you feel ready for it, come on back to it. I've pointed out some of the "tricks" to listen for, i.e. trills, octave splits, slides and growls. These are covered in detail later on the cassette.

Note that when an arc covers a few notes ⌢ it means those notes are to be slurred together and played very quickly. Also note the following quirk in the tab: as you already know, when a bent note is to be played it will be notated with a bent arrow (2) but

when <u>only</u> the <u>bent</u> or flatted part of that note is to be played it will be notated with a "straight/bent" arrow (2) OK?

BACKUP HARP

Take a listen to Little Walter playing with Muddy Waters, and to Sonny Terry on songs sung by Brownie McGhee. Their backup playing is a lesson unto itself.

In the simplest of terms, you can try the following on a 3-chord blues:

trill holes 3 and 4 draw on the I chord;

trill holes 4 and 5 blow on the IV chord;

trill holes 4 and 5 draw on the V chord;

at the final part of the turnaround, hit hole 1 draw.

Also, try simply hitting the backbeat in a "chunk/chunk" fashion. If you're playing with a drummer, listen for the backbeat (it's the 2 and 4 of a 1-2-3-4 count.) In a bluegrass format, the backbeat is usually picked up by the mandolin player. Above all, don't be soloing during the verses (unless it's your solo.) Know when to lay out entirely. Harmonica (like, say, banjo) can be downright obnoxious when overplayed, or played on the wrong song. For some tunes it doesn't work at all, so know when to say when.

Photo Courtesy of Mary Katherine Aldin

Willie Dixon, Sonny Terry, Brownie McGhee

31

LICKS

Now we get into the meat of the matter. Listen along to the cassette while you look these over.

1. The "I'm a Man" Style Lick

(Note that I played this slightly differently the first time than I did the second and third...)

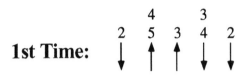

1st Time:

```
        4       3
    2   5   3   4   2
    ↓   ↑   ↑   ↓   ↓
```

2nd and 3rd Time:

```
        4   3
    2   5   4   2
    ↓   ↑   ↓   ↓
```

2. The Boogie Beat

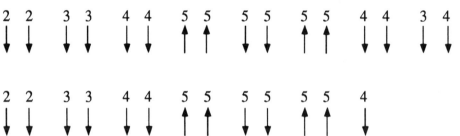

```
2  2   3  3   4  4   5  5   5  5   5  5   4  4   3  4
↓  ↓   ↓  ↓   ↓  ↓   ↑  ↑   ↓  ↓   ↑  ↑   ↓  ↓   ↓  ↓

2  2   3  3   4  4   5  5   5  5   5  5   4
↓  ↓   ↓  ↓   ↓  ↓   ↑  ↑   ↓  ↓   ↑  ↑   ↓
```

3. The Stop-Time Lick

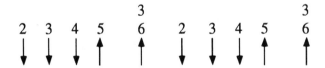

```
                3               3
    2  3  4  5  6   2  3  4  5  6
    ↓  ↓  ↓  ↑  ↑   ↑  ↓  ↓  ↓  ↑  ↑
```

Note that the final chord of this lick is a tongue-block (or "octave split.") This technique also came up during the solo on the 4th verse of the 12 bar blues, and is discussed later on the cassette. Basically, it involves blowing holes 3 and 6, but not 4 and 5. This is achieved by blocking out holes 4 and 5 with the tongue. The easiest way to do it is to actually aim the tongue for the post between holes 4 and 5, and touch it to the lower part of that post.

32

4. The "Help Me" Lick

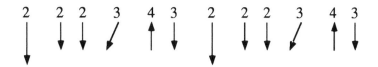

Try to get a partial bend and a growl on the 4th note of this lick.

5. The Up Lick

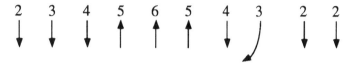

Note the long bend on note #8 (3-draw.)

6. The Circle Lick

This lick is much easier than it sounds. The first thing to do is work hard on bending hole #4. First work on bending it downward from it's normal pitch, but then concentrate on <u>pre-bending</u> it and releasing it up to it's normal pitch. Once you've mastered pre-bending hole #4, immediately move the harp over slightly to hole #5. Those are the main notes to this lick:

Now, simply repeat these notes over and over again until you can speed them up.

7. An Ending Lick

Note that the first 3 chords are octave-splits

Again, a "straight/bent" arrow ( as opposed to) designates you are to hit only the bent section of that note (as in notes 6, 9, 14.)
The last note is a drastically bent #2 draw.

8. Introduction Lick

```
1 2 1   2 1 2 1 2 1   3
4 5 4   5 4 5 4 5 4   6   5 5 4 3 2
↓ ↑ ↓   ↓ ↓ ↓ ↓ ↓ ↓   ↑   ↓ ↑ ↓ ↓ ↓

3 4 4 4   4 3 2 2   1 1 1 1
↓ ↑ ↓ ↓   ↓ ↓ ↓ ↓   ↓ ↓ ↓ ↓
```

BREATHING/PHRASING

This is one area in which beginning harp players make things tougher than necessary on themselves. For example when you hear a very fast lick consisting of many quick notes, there is often an incorrect assumption that this lick must have many changes of wind direction-and that's almost never the case.

To illustrate, take a listen to the "Fast Draw" lick at the end of side A. It is a fast and complex lick, consisting of bent and unbent notes, but the <u>entire</u> lick is performed on <u>draw</u> notes. Here's the way this lick maps out:

FAST DRAW LICK:

As you can see, this lick consists of bent and unbent draw notes, all slurred together. Breathing is really never a concern, since the whole lick is performed with one long and sustained inward breath.

Try to resist the temptation to think of each note played as requiring a <u>separate</u> breath. A player is almost never required to switch wind direction with every note, so breathing and phrasing are usually situations which sort themselves out.

Since #2 draw is the root note, and since the other draw notes near it (#1-6) fit nicely into the blues scale, you're going to be inhaling about 80% of the time. The only possible problem with this is that your lungs may fill up with air, and you'll have to stop for a moment to blow (or sing) it out.

In such a case, remember that #3 blow is the <u>same</u> note as #2 draw... and we all know that #2 draw is the root, right? Therefore, you always have a safety valve: if you need wind (either way) you can always either blow out through #3, or draw in through #2. (Be careful <u>only</u> to hit one hole at a time, though.) This may not be the most musically articulate way to solve the problem, but it sure works.

In workshops I am often asked "Since you shift so much between singing and harp, you must have a lot of wind, right?"

Some folks are surprised to hear that the answer is no... with this style of playing, it's actually easier to shift quickly back and forth between vocal and harp. That's because the primary wind direction with blues harp is to inhale; and of course we exhale when we sing. So, if in between vocal lines you see me go quickly to the harp, I'm really just sucking up some wind through it (and hopefully also making some musical sense!)

The only time any of this becomes a problem is if you're gigging at high altitude. Many years ago Kenny and I did a 3 night stand at Whiskey Creek, in Mammoth, and on the first night I was seeing flashcubes from hyperventilation. So if you live in Hunza or Tibet, take it easy and lay off the cheap stogies.

OVERBLOWING

This is a relatively new technique, pioneered by an Illinois musician named Howard Levy. Although not often heard in blues, and mastered by very few, this technique is so revolutionary that it demands inclusion in any discussion of the diatonic harmonica.

First of all, practice this only on an old harp. Until you get a feel for it, you might just blow out a new harp by practicing it. Find an old C-harp and blow on hole #6 - you get a G note. Now, purse your lips together like a bugler and really <u>blow</u>! What should result is that the note will "crack" upward, becoming a (somewhat froggy sounding) note that is a step and a half <u>higher</u> in pitch than normal (it's a Bb.) This is an overblow.

Each hole is capable of an overblow to some degree. Somehow, Howard Levy figured out both how to control this strange phenomenon, and how to incorporate it into his playing. In theory, it's possible to overblow #1 - 6 on any key harp, but players who use this technique tell me it is easiest on holes #4, 5 and 6, and also very difficult on high-keyed harps (E, F, F#.) In any event, an expanded range of notes becomes available.

Howard Levy's own playing is completely unique and incorporates all the advantages of chromatic playing while retaining the bendability and tone of the diatonic. If you really want to feel like a dinosaur, (I sure do!) check out Howard's work on recordings by Bela Fleck and the Flecktones, or go see them live. I guarantee you'll be shaking your head in astonishment... this guy's truly the mad scientist of the harmonica!

PLAYING WITH A GUITARIST

Harp and guitar go together like baseball and hot dogs. There is a long standing tradition of duos playing these instruments, and there are literally thousands of recordings ranging from early partnerships like Bobby Leecan and Robert Cooksey to contemporary teams like John Cephas and Phil Wiggins. In the overwhelming majority of cases, the harmonica will play cross harp (2nd position.) The challenges for the guitarist are many, as some guitar keys lend themselves more easily to blues than others. Due to the presence of open strings, the keys of E and A are particularly good for guitar blues; C and G also work well for the Piedmont style of raggier blues.

This matters little to the harpist, of course, as he can simply play different harps to fit different keys. But if the harpist is also the vocalist, then one's vocal range enters the picture...that's where a capo comes in handy.

In my own partnership with guitarist Kenny Sultan, we play in almost every key. Fortunately for me, Kenny is an extremely fluent player in every position, but there are occasions where the capo can be a life saver: E-flat, for instance.

Another potential problem is tuning: some harps are out of tune with each other. This means the guitar and harp can be perfectly in tune for a song in E, but then slightly out for the next song in G. Since you can't tune your harp, it is the guitar that must repeatedly make the on-stage adjustments. Here's what my partner Kenny has to say to blues guitarists about playing with a harp blower:

"What I try to do, basically, is to tune my guitar to one central harmonica, C for example, and then don't worry too much about minor fluctuations. If the harp is really out of tune you have three choices: do nothing, retune your whole guitar, or make small adjustments to the tonic notes. Generally, you're never going to be in perfect tune, considering the nature of the music and the nature of both instruments -bent strings, bent notes, etc. So just try to get it close and have some fun."

King Biscuit Boys in the studios of KFFA - 1944

Joe Willie Wilkens   Joe "Pine Top" Perkins   Sonny Boy Williamson   Mr. Hugh Smith Announcer   James "Peck" Curtis   Houston Stackhouse

L.R. Tom Ball, George Thorogood, Kenny Sultan, 1986

Photo by Debbie Stuettig - Triplett

PLAYING WITH A RACK

In a word: difficult. I started trying to play with a rack in the early '60s in an attempt to accompany myself on guitar, ala Bob Dylan. At the time there were no commercially made harmonica racks (at least not in my neighborhood,) so my pals and I used to bend them out of coat hangers. Today there are a couple different rack designs available, but the difficulties of mastering the technique itself are unchanged.

Simply breathing through the harp while playing guitar, ala Dylan, is relatively easy. But to really play the thing that way is another ball of wax. The most obvious problem with rack work is that one's hands are tied up playing the guitar, and therefore not free to work the harp. This means that techniques like tremolo, hand smacks, wah-wahs, etc., are no longer possible. The player must try to compensate with a strong throat vibrato.

Also, trills cannot now be accomplished by the usual method of wobbling the harp back and forth in the mouth. Instead, the player must wobble his head. Rapid movements of the head cause the shoulders to shift, moving the harp rack, so pretty soon you find yourself chasing your harmonica all around.

And then there are also problems of coordination, for while you're battling all this you're also theoretically trying to play the guitar. And sing too, maybe. Jeez, ya gotta be Sybil to pull it all off. All can say is thank God for multi-track recording studios.

Two of the best rack players around are Dr. Isiah Ross and John Hammond. By all means, check these two out in concert, and look for recordings by the late Slim Harpo and the late, great Jimmy Reed. Good luck, and remember it helps to be schizophrenic.

RIFFS AND TRICKS

The following riffs and tricks are discussed, played and analyzed on Side B of the accompanying cassette:

TREMOLO

WAH-WAH

TRILLS

SHAKES

VIBRATO

OCTAVE SPLITTING

GROWLS

SLIDES

SLAPPING

CHUGGING

CUTTING OFF THE NOTE

TONGUE TRILLS

THROAT POPS

CAR HORN

Since nearly all of these techniques involve the altering of a given tone, they therefore do not translate into tablature... And since all this is covered so thoroughly on the cassette, it is my feeling that to simply repeat the discussion verbatim here in print would be redundant.

However, I do not wish to underestimate the importance of these techniques. It is my hope that students will pay very close attention to that section of the tape.

There is one exception to the above, though, and that is the technique known as "chugging." Below you will find the tab for the first part of what I play on the cassette. (A-harp.)

Chugging:

```
          1   1       2      1   1               1   1       2      1   1
          2   2       3      2   2           2   2       3      2   2
      2   3   3       4      3   3       2   3   3       4      3   3           2
      ↓   ↓   ↓       ↑      ↓   ↓       ↓   ↓   ↓       ↑      ↓   ↓           ↓
```

With the 1 chords coming in such rapid succession,

```
      2
      3
      ↓
```

don't actually take a separate breath for each one... rather, practice bouncing the tongue off the roof of the mouth in order to supply a more percussive effect. And by all means, pick up some Sonny Terry albums!

39

OTHER POSITIONS

In effect, when we refer to positions we are referring to modes.

FIRST POSITION

is "straight harp," i.e. a C-harmonica being played in the key of C. The #4 blow is the central note, or root. (See chapter on straight harp.) This is also called "Ionian mode."

SECOND POSITION

has also already been covered... it is "cross harp," in which a C-harmonica is played in the key of G. The #2 draw is the root note, and the overwhelming emphasis is on draw notes and bent notes. <u>This is by far the most important, most played and most often heard position for blues harp.</u> My own style consists of 90% cross harp; Sonny Terry played exclusively in this position. (For all you theorists, this is "Mixolydian mode.")

Though I use them only rarely in my playing with Kenny, it would be an injustice not to at least touch upon the other positions that are possible with a diatonic harp. On occasion the phone rings and I'll be called to a non-blues recording session...then it can be trial by fire! These other positions can be very handy alternatives, particularly for popular music in minor keys.

THIRD POSITION

or "Minor Dorian," is where your C-harp plays in D-minor. You take the #1 draw as your root note. (Technically, the available scale in this position isn't strictly minor: the third and seventh are minor, but the sixth is major.) Of all the "higher" positions, this one will probably come in the handiest. Little Walter played some wonderful stuff in third position - some of his jazzy sounding minor-key instrumentals were achieved this way.

FOURTH POSITION

("Phrygian") is where (on a C-harp) you make the #2 blow (E) the tonic, or root. Now you're working in E-minor with a flatted second.

FIFTH POSITION

("Aeolian") is centered around #6 draw, and is an A-minor natural scale (on a C-harp.)

There is also (theoretically) a **SIXTH POSITION** ("Lydian") where you play in F on a C-harp; and a **SEVENTH POSITION** ("Locrian") where you play in B on a C-harp. But I've never actually heard anybody use these positions... nor do I think I want to.

Sometimes it becomes necessary to change harps several times during the course of a song, particularly if the song modulates in key and/or changes modes. During one memorable recording session I did for a multiple Grammy-award-winning composer, I was forced to change harps 55 different times during one song!

If all this stuff confuses you, welcome to the club! Even as I write this, I'm on my way to the medicine cabinet for a couple aspirins. For the purposes of blues harmonica (after all, that's the title of this book,) you need only concern yourself for now with cross harp.

HOW TO PRODUCE
"SCOTCH BAGPIPE" EFFECT

Use a "Little Lady" Harmonica. (A Harmonica with four holes, in the key of A.) This trick should be presented with the assistance of a violinist.

The violinist plays a steady drone on the "A" string, gradually taking the time of the Harmonica player.

Place the little Harmonica well into your mouth. Play some simple Scotch ballad, like "The Campbells' Are Coming." By repeating it two or three times and always ending on the highest note of the Harmonica the bagpipe effect can be produced.

NON-STANDARD TUNINGS

So far, everything we've discussed and/or played has been under the assumption that we've been using a harmonica in the standard (or Richter) tuning.   But there are a few other choices worth mentioning.

Major 7th Tuning ("COUNTRY TUNING") C-Harp

	1	2	3	4	5	6	7	8	9	10
BLOW	C	E	G	C	E	G	C	E	G	C
DRAW	D	G	B	D	F#	A	B	D	F	A

If you back up to the chapter on straight harp and compare this diagram to that one, you'll see the only difference here is hole 5 draw. It is now a half-step sharper, enabling the player to hit what is a previously unattainable F#.

The major 7th is not an essential harp, but it comes in handy now and then if a song is in an odd mode. I don't know why it's called "country tuning," though... in my experience, most country songs utilize standard tuned harp, if any...

I must admit I haven't spent alot of time exploring this harp's potential, but many fine players swear by this arrangement. Steve Baker, in his superb work *The Harp Handbook*, says "The major 7th tuning opens up an enormous range of new musical possibilities, without requiring that you master overblowing ... I would never be without them."

Sonny Terry

MINOR AND OTHER TUNINGS

Both Hohner and Lee Oscar market a couple of different minor-tuned configurations, called harmonic minor and natural minor. Frankly I'm pretty ignorant about these harps, since I hardly ever have to play in a minor key; and if I do, I just change positions... Additionally, there are all sorts of custom and exotic tunings which can be special-ordered from Hohner, I would invite anyone interested in a more thorough discussion to get ahold of the previously mentioned *Harp Handbook* by Steve Baker (distributed by Hohner,) Steve probably knows more about the diatonic harp than anyone else alive. I don't want to sound like an advertisement, but this is one very special book - and in it there is an enormous chapter devoted to different tunings. Check it out.

Howard Levy

PLAYING ALONG WITH RECORDS

This is without doubt the most underrated of all learning tools associated with playing the blues harmonica. Harp is one of those instruments that's difficult to practice alone. Unlike guitar or piano, a harp's not exactly self-contained - and practicing it becomes much easier if you're playing along with someone...

Which is all fine and dandy if you happen to have a good guitarist for a roommate or a blues band living downstairs, but not everyone is so fortunate. And in addition, hearing a good harp player while you're practicing makes it all the easier. That's why playing along with records is so important.

In fact, I recommend to students that for <u>every hour you spend practicing, spend at least 2 hours listening</u>. Try to completely surround yourself with blues harp music. After awhile you begin to absorb that sound; certain licks will get stuck in your brain. The underlying chord changes in the song structures will eventually become second nature, and all the theoretical analysis will seem irrelevant because you'll be able to play blues changes in your sleep!

So....which recordings should you play along with? The obvious choices would be the acknowledged masters: Sonny Terry, Little Walter, Sonnyboy Williamson II, etc. In the Appendix "A" is a complete rundown of essential recordings. But in addition to these, try to pick up all of Muddy Waters' early stuff. Although Muddy was a guitarist, there is perhaps more good harmonica blowing on his recordings than anywhere else.

When playing along with records, it is <u>essential</u> that you determine what key a song is in, then use the appropriate harp. At this stage <u>don't worry about any position other than cross harp</u> (2nd position.)

If you just grab the first harp you see and then try to play along with a recording, you only stand a one in twelve chance of having the correct harp. This can frustrate the hell out of a beginner, because even the wrong key harp will occasionally spit out a few "'right" notes by sheer coincidence; and then the player, who now wrongly assumes the harp is correct, finds himself unable to locate many of the notes the recorded harpist is playing.

So, first of all, <u>determine the key</u>. How do you do that? If you also happen to play guitar, simply play every fret on the high E string until you find the root note (assuming your guitar is in tune.) If you don't play another instrument, you may have to find somebody who does and ask them to figure it out for you. It only takes a second - it's very simple. Once the key has been determined, go back to the "cross harp" discussion and look at the chart to find out which harp to use. (Better still, memorize that chart!) Now you're ready to honk along.

There's only one other thing that can mess up your mind, and that's pitch. It helps to have a pitch control device on your turntable or cassette deck. A lot of tape decks run slightly slow or fast, throwing off the pitch a little. What's more, some older recordings were actually cut a bit fast or slow. The result is that some blues records seem as though they're kind of "in between" two keys, which can lead to Excedrin Headache #666. If necessary, you may have to have your tape deck serviced and/or adjusted.

Now, assuming your machinery is in order, and you've got the right key harp and a few good recordings, it's time to go to town!

Start playing along. Draw hole 2 and you've got the root. Concentrate on draw notes; in fact, you'll want to inhale 80% of the time. Stay on the bottom 6 holes for now, and you'll find yourself (maybe accidentally) playing some of the stuff the recorded harpist is playing. If Little Walter hits a particularly cool lick, stop your machine and try to find it on your harp. Figuring out how the masters do what they do is terrific ear-training. Later, of course, you'll want to establish a style of your own, but for now it's perfectly OK to swipe shamelessly. Happy larceny.

PHYSICS

Diatonic harps are quirky little beasts, and actually work somewhat differently than one would expect. For years I was at a loss to explain why, for example, my #4 blow reeds were always the first to go flat due to metal fatigue. It didn't seem logical; after all, I hardly ever played (and can't bend) #4 blow. Why then was it always the first to break down?

Then one day Fred Palmer explained to me a bit about the physics of the harp and a few years later Steve Baker wrote the definative chapter on the subject. I am indebted to both these gentlemen for bringing me out of the dark ages.

When a player blows through a hole, there is the assumption that all the wind is traveling outward through the blow reed slit; conversely, one assumes that when drawing, the air is only entering through the draw reed slit. Wrong.

If you take a harp apart you find there is nothing inside to direct the airflow thusly. In reality when blowing, your wind is actually going out through both the draw and blow reed slits; and when drawing, the wind enters through both slits. Other than making us all work a little harder than necessary, this has virtually no effect on the tone or sound - that is, until one begins to bend (or overblow) notes.

The physical phenomenon of bending is more complex than it seems. The term would suggest simply that the reed bends and unbends in conjunction with the note itself; but this is not strictly the case.

When a player draws in through a hole and bends that note downward in pitch, several things take place inside the harp. At the beginning of the bend, the draw reed is producing the tone, as expected. As the bend becomes deeper in pitch, however, the blow reed begins to vibrate sympathetically. Finally, at the deepest part of the bend, the draw reed virtually ceases to vibrate at all, and the tone is now almost entirely the result of the <u>blow</u> reed (vibrating <u>higher</u> than it's given pitch.) It is the two reeds interacting like this that allows us the deep "bluesy" bends.

The same principle occurs in reverse with regard to the high-note blow-bends. And, strangely enough it comes into play again with regard to overblows (it is actually the <u>draw</u> reed which controls the overblow tone.)

With a chromatic harp, windsaver valves are attached to the reeds. These valves are designed to stop blow reeds from functioning during a draw, and stop draw reeds from functioning during a blow, supposedly to save the player's wind. The net result, however, is to inhibit the bendability by preventing the 2 reeds from working in conjunction. Bottom line: no deep bends on a chromatic.

MAINTENANCE AND REPAIR

Back when a Marine Band cost $1.89, a player could afford to ignore maintenance and repair - but in today's economy it makes alot of sense to try to prolong the life span of your instruments.

First thing to realize is that no matter what you do, your harps won't last forever. The harder you play them and the more you bend the reeds, the faster they give out, so it's best just to accept that fact up front.

Having said that, though, there are some things you can do to avoid the premature demise of your loved ones. First of all, keep 'em clean! Harps get full of all kinds of weird Chicken Delight, so every now and then it's wise to take' em apart and give' em a good scrub. I usually use a toothpick to scrape off all the unidentifiable gunk and an emery board for the rust. Then I rub the cover plates, inside and out, with alcohol. When you take your harp apart, be careful not to bend the cover plates. If you do, you'll wreck the airtightness of the harp, making it harder to play.

With a Marine Band, be advised that the little screws holding down the cover plates are actually rivets disguised as screws... so don't waste your time trying to unscrew them. And when you put the plates back on, don't use your teeth to drive in the rivets! I have 5 chipped teeth directly attributable to harp repair combined with the impatience of youth. Dental bills cost more than harps.

Keep them in their case when you're not playing them. Sucking a harp-load of lint, sand, or tobacco flakes isn't a happy proposition. And if you keep them in your back pocket, don't sit on 'em... you'll squish the cover plates and hurt your heinie. And, as Tony Glover says, "Don't drop them in the toilet or let anyone with bubonic plague play them."

SOAKING HARPS

Do yourself a favor: don't soak your harps. Soaking a harp wrecks it in the long run.

The premise for soaking harps is that it supposedly makes them louder and easier to play. With a wooden comb harp, the wood will swell, making the harp more airtight. This increases compression and theoretically facilitates ease of play.

The downside, however, is that as soon as the harp dries out it's even harder to play than it was before you soaked it. Also, the wood will swell to the point where it's protruding from the harp's face, and the entire guts of the harp immediately begin to rust. Plus, soaked harps go out of tune faster. The paint peels, the wood warps... welcome to the garbage can.

Soaking plastic combed harps is even more absurd, since whatever limited advantage soaking can provide is negated by the fact that plastic doesn't react in water like wood does.

The only time it might be appropriate to get your harp wet is if it's on it's last legs. Every now and then I'll run an old harp under some cold tap water, just to try to squeeze one more gig out of it. But think of it only as a last resort.

SHAVING

Even if you don't soak your harps, your wooden comb harp will eventually swell if you play it enough. This means the little posts of the comb may begin to protrude from the harp's face, making it uncomfortable to play. In that case, get yourself a razor blade and start shaving. But remember to shave up and down rather than side to side, so the posts don't move around or bust off. Some people use sandpaper for this operation, but then they suck up a lot of sawdust... myself, I just use a plastic comb Special 20 and don't worry about it.

MINOR SURGERY

Most minor problems are of the stuck reed variety. You're playing along without a care when suddenly a note simply refuses to sound - you've got a stuck reed.

Open up your harp and locate the problem. Remember the blow reeds are on top, draw reeds the bottom. Chances are some piece of foreign material is caught in the reed, preventing it from vibrating. Poking around with a toothpick ought to fix that.

Occasionally the problem will be with the reed itself. Sometimes one will get stuck in it's channel and need to be freed, or, less often, the degree of offset needs adjusting. If the angle of the offending reed is noticeably different than that of all the other reeds, try to gently adjust it with a toothpick until it matches the others.

TERMINAL BREAKDOWN

Harps fade out in a variety of ways. The most common cause of death is metal fatigue, which results in a flattening of the pitch in one or more of the reeds. This is because reeds are made out of brass, not the world's hardest metal. There has been some experimentation with stainless steel reeds, but stainless steel turns out to be too rigid (and too rust prone.) You'd have to be a human vacuum cleaner to bend a stainless steel reed.

If you're playing your harmonica without accompaniment or simply using it to practice your bending technique, then it's probably not that bothersome if one reed is slightly flat - but once you begin playing with other musicians the problem becomes painfully evident.

Every harpist plays in a different fashion, which means his or her harps will break down in a different way. As we discussed in "Physics," it is a quirk of the harp that on a deep draw bend, the corresponding <u>blow</u> reed is the one that comes under the most stress. In my case, I tend to ride the 4 draw bend alot, which means that the #4 blow reed is usually the first one to flatten out. The result is a sour chord. At this point I've got two choices: either throw the sucker out or try to retune it.

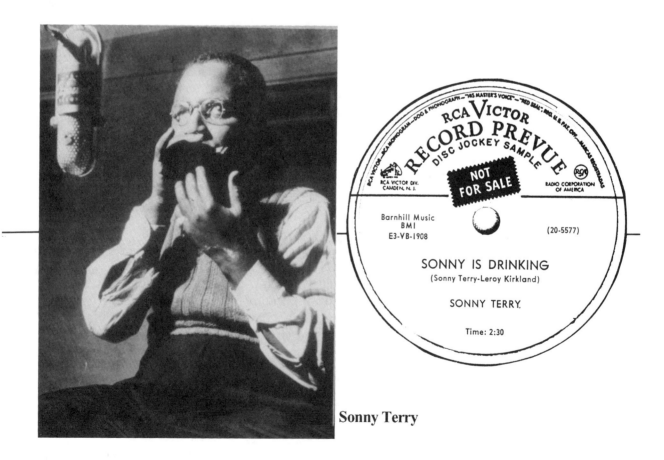

Sonny Terry

MAJOR SURGERY
TUNING YOUR HARPS

Think of this as the final resort. You may well kill your harp trying this procedure, so practice it a few times on harps already destined for the dung heap.

First locate the offending reed. Then elevate it slightly with a toothpick and slide a razor blade underneath it as a sort of "worktable." It's probably best to use a blade that's not quite as rusty as the one shown. (Photo #1)

Now you'll need a small jeweler's file (or a good nail file). If the pitch has gone flat (most common) you will want to raise the pitch by taking a bit of weight off the tip of the reed. (Important: do not actually try to shorten the reed. The reed should stay the same length it is already!)

With the file, lightly take a few swipes diagonally across the reed at the tip (photo #2.) Again, the object is not to file the reed shorter. Only do 2 or 3 swipes, then remove the razor blade and test the pitch. Repeat this procedure until the reed is in tune, being careful not to overcorrect to the point that the reed's now too sharp!

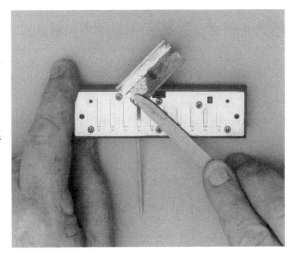

In the case of a reed that is too sharp (very rare) you can lower the pitch by scratching lightly across the reed (diagonally) back by where it is riveted to the reed plate, about 1/4 of the way out. (Photo #3)

> **Tuning your harp in this fashion can be both time consuming and frustrating. What's more, there is no guarantee - even if you do manage to get your harp back into perfect tune, there's at least a 50/50 chance that as soon as you start playing it hard, it'll go flat again due to metal fatigue.**

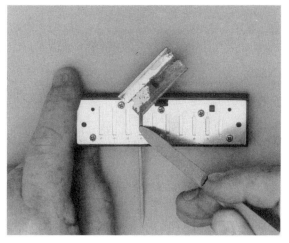

TRANSPLANTS

If your harp does expire on the operating table, don't bury it - save the body parts for future transplant surgery. Extra cover plates, in particular, come in handy down the road. Have yourself an Irish wake, then drop on down to the music store for a little reincarnation therapy.

Sonny Boy Williamson

Photo Courtesy Chess/MCA

DANCE & PARTY

At _____

Date _____

Time _____

IN PERSON

2 BIG

TRUMPET

STARS

"SONNY BOY" WILLIAMSON

" Mighty Long Time " · " Nine Below Zero " · " Pontiac Blues " · " Mr. Down Child " · " Stop Crying "

ELMO JAMES

Singing His Current Big Hit - " Dust My Broom " And Others

☆ ☆☆ ☆☆ ☆

Photo by Larry Sultan

Tom Ball and Kenny Sultan, Kenny, please check out that sign in back of your head.

48

ELECTRIC BLUES

Amplified harmonica began to surface in the late '40s and found it's way onto records by the early '50s. The approach is somewhat different than playing acoustic blues, and although many riffs are played in the same way, the resulting sound is hugely different.

Take a listen to Little Walter's early acoustic work with the Muddy Waters band. On tunes like "Louisiana Blues," for example, or "Evans Shuffle" (both from 1950,) Walter's playing is very "country." That is to say the approach is acoustic, involves much handwork and has none of the sweeping saxophone-like quality that marked his later recordings. This is not to criticize his playing, for his work on these two tunes is brilliant, just that it lacks the Little Walter tone we are accustomed to hearing.

Now take a listen to Walter's playing on Muddy's "She Moves Me" (1951) or on Walter's own recording of "Juke" (1952.) The sound is completely different, and this difference is the very definition and essence of the Chicago-style harp sound. Virtually overnight, Walter Jacobs (together with Walter Horton and Junior Wells) changed the sound, the role and the expectations of the instrument- in much the same manner as when Charlie Christian, T-Bone Walker and Les Paul had changed the direction of the guitar by amplifying it a decade earlier.

In James Rooney's book *Bossmen*, Muddy talked about Little Walter: "He had a thing on the harp that nobody had. And today they're still trying for it, but they can't come up to it. It really fitted in with me, what I was doing and he was much younger than me, but he could really understand the blues and he knew what to put in there and when to put it in there. So all I can say is that he is the greatest I've ever heard."

The shape of things to come: Little Walter's first record, 1947

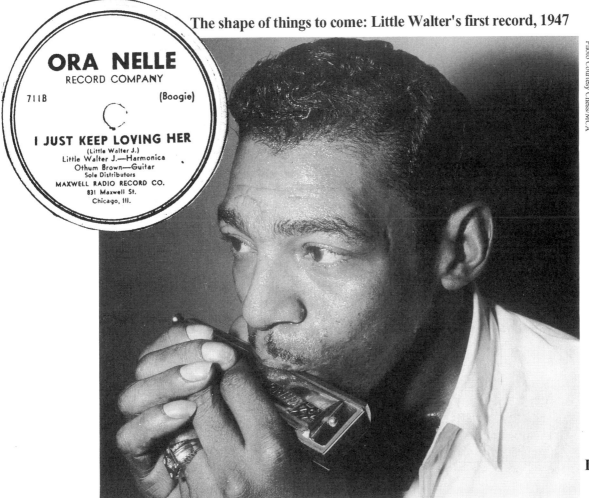

Photo Courtesy Chess/MCA

Little Walter

Considering that some of the other folks Muddy played with (formally or informally) included both Sonnyboy Williamsons, Walter Horton, Junior Wells, George Smith, Henry Strong, James Cotton, Paul Butterfield and many more, the "greatest I've ever heard" quote takes on real significance.

AMPLIFIERS

There are as many ways to amplify a harp as there are amplifiers and mikes. One good way to avoid sounding like geese farts on a rainy day is to avoid solid-state amps like the plague. They're incapable of providing the warm, distorted tone color that is the corner-stone of the amplified blues sound. Stick to tube amps.

Of all the tube amp arrangements, in the eyes of many players the ultimate would be a vintage tweed Fender 4x10 Bassman (together with a Fender reverb tank.) The problem is that vintage 4x10s have become ridiculously expensive, as they are also highly sought after by guitarists and (shudder) collectors. A few years ago you could have picked one up for a reasonable price, but those days are long gone.

Each to his own tastes, however. I once saw Howlin' Wolf blowing through what appeared to be an old record player. Although many harpists swear by the 4x10 Bassman, there are others who are less convinced - my buddy James Harman among them.

"Over the years I've owned 13 of 'em," James recently told me, "but I sold every one. Just really didn't like 'em. When I try to play through them I start makin' faces, man... but then, I'm an oddball." So how does Harman get his superb tone? "A '63 brown Fender Vibroverb, with a 15" Jensen instead of the 2 10" Oxfords." He also uses a custom made preamp. The results are spacious; this cat is <u>bad</u>.

Virtually any pre-CBS tweed or blackface Fender is worth trying out. Among the other popular models are the Reverb, Super Reverb, Pro Reverb, Deluxe Reverb and Princeton Reverb.

Some of these amps may not be loud enough for a large room, in which case you can dangle a mike in front of the amp and feed the signal into the P.A., a situation which also enables you to make some EQ adjustments right on the board if necessary.

I have seen some harp blowers use other tube amps (not Fenders) with varying re-sults, mostly vintage Gibsons, Epiphones, Silvertones and the like. A late-'50s Gibson GA 18 Explorer, for example, can offer a fat warm sound without breaking the bank. The Epis and Silvertones are less successful, but they will give you a really grungy sound if that's all you're after. Modern amps like Marshall, Peavey, Ampeg, etc., don't cut it at all for blues harp.

When it comes to effects, the only one you really need is reverb. Some salesmen will try to convince you that digital delay or echo is "the same thing as reverb." It ain't. Don't believe 'em. Other built-in amp effects (vibrato, tremolo, etc.,) are superfluous and will go largely unused, but reverb is a necessity (and plenty of it.)

The ideal situation would be to find an early '60s Fender outboard reverb unit, sometimes called a "reverb tank." These babies allow you to adjust the tone and dwell of the 'verb, and are better and warmer sounding than the reverb that's built into any amp. What's more, if you have this independent re-verb source you won't then have to limit yourself to buying an amp with built-in reverb. Instead, you'll be able to pick from the better, even older tweed Fender amps that do <u>not</u> have built-in 'verb. (i.e. the 4x10 Bassman, Deluxe, Pro, etc.)

Incidentally, if you want to accurately date your older Fender amp, take a peek at the amp's tube chart. There should be a two-letter code stamped in ink on it. The first letter signifies the year, the second signifies the month. Following on the next page is the translation.

FIRST LETTER	SECOND LETTER
A = 1951	A = January
B = 1952	B = February
C = 1953	C = March
D = 1954	D = April
E = 1955	E = May
F = 1956	F = June
G = 1957	G = July
H = 1958	H = August
I = 1959	I = September
J = 1960	J = October
K = 1961	K = November
L = 1962	L = December
M = 1963	
N = 1964	
0 = 1965	
P = 1966	
Q = 1967	

Examples: GC =March, 1957. NJ =October, 1964

If the tube chart is missing, try checking the 6-digit code painted on the speaker rim. (This sometimes works for dating non-Fenders as well. Only works, though, if the speaker is original.)

The first three numbers signify the speaker manufacturer:

220 =Jensen. 465 =Oxford. 328 =Utah/Oxford.

The fourth digit corresponds to the last digit of the year of manufacture:

2 = 1952 or 1962. 9 = 1949 or 1959.

The final 2 numbers are the week of manufacture.

Example: 465210 is an Oxford speaker made in the 10th week of either 1952 or 1962.

Before we move on, a short word about reissue amps: in the last few years, Fender (as well as Kendricks and a couple of other companies) has issued a repro 4x10 Bassman amp. Although it fails to exactly capture the warmth and tone of the original, with a few minor adjustments it is pretty damn close and goes for about 1/4 the money. A very utilitarian option, and it also doubles great as a guitar amp. Extremely loud! But don't forget the reverb tank, and keep in mind you'd have to be Arnold Schwarzenegger to carry the sucker around.

Brownie McGhee and Sonny Terry (with road crew) England, 1964

MICROPHONES

A lot of electric players simply blow through any available P.A. mike, an approach which fails to take advantage of an amp's full potential. Ideally with electric blues, the player is singing through one mike and blowing through another. Let's take a look at a typical set-up:

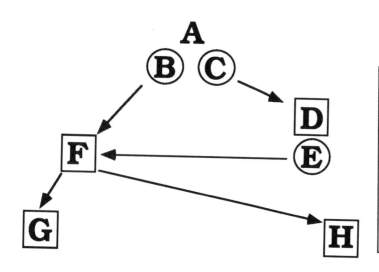

A=harmonica player/singer (you!)
B=vocal mike on a stand (for singing)
C=hand-held harp mike
D=amplifier (for harp)
E=mike suspended in front of harp amp
F=P.A. head/mixing board
G–P.A. speaker
H=P.A. speaker

Here we have a good scenario. In this manner the vocal can remain clean while the harp is achieving the bluesy, muddy tone it so richly deserves. (Incidentally, I usually have my amp settings very bassy...you'll probably find you'll want the treble down and the bass up, otherwise the harp tends to sound strident.)

The best mikes for the Chicago-style amplified harp sound are the Shure 520 D (aka the "green bullet,") Astatic JT-30, and/or the Hohner Blues Blaster 1490. All are small, hand held bullet-shaped mikes originally designed for ham radio. These are the kind of mikes Broderick Crawford yelled "ten-four!" into, on *Highway Patrol.*

The green bullet (Shure 520 D) was originally issued decades ago, then reappeared in a slightly altered form in the early '80s. Old "silver bullets" also exist. This mike is larger than the Astatic (or Hohner,) and is a dynamic microphone (i.e. a moving-coil type.) It is sturdy, sensitive and loud. At high volume, however, it faithfully amplifies the obnoxious sound of the harp scraping across the grill, and it is also prone to feedback.

The Astatic JT-30 is a crystal mike from roughly the same era, and is my personal favorite. It's a bit smaller and lighter than the Shure, and you can't beat the sound. In his book *Microphones - How they Work and How To Use Them*, Martin Clifford says "If you want a microphone for fun and games and for partying, and you aren't concerned with sound quality, there's nothing wrong with using a crystal microphone." Hmmm... in other words, it's perfect for blues.

Hohner's Blues Blaster 1490 is, in effect, a repackaged Astatic JT-30 with a volume control. As I haven't tried one of these yet, I don't feel qualified to comment... but I have heard good reports from other players.

As with harps, mike and amp choice is purely a matter of personal preference. Go see somebody whose tone you like and, on the break ask them what they're using. Better still, buy 'em a beer first, then ask.

My own current amplified harp set up is an Astatic JT-30 to a late '62 Fender reverb tank to a '56 Fender tweed Deluxe. If necessary, I'll mike the amp into the P.A.

For the last word on electric harp, I'd like to quote Steve Baker again from his indispensable *Harp Handbook*: "A great electric setup does not necessarily guarantee you a great sound in itself - the acoustic tone of the player is the most important single factor. I would recommend anyone who's into electric harp to practice at developing a good acoustic sound too, rather than hoping that the volume and distortion will cover up any failings. All the good electric players have a good acoustic tone on which they build." Amen, brother.

PS - On the accompanying cassette there is a very brief lick, used as an example to show the difference between acoustic and electric tones.

For those of you who might be interested, here is that lick in tab:

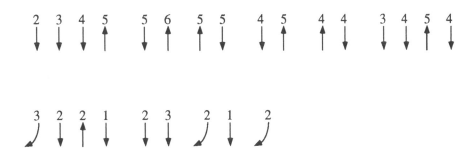

Little Walter

INDISCRETION STOMP

By Tom Ball and Kenny Sultan
Flying Fish Music, BMI

From "Bloodshot Eyes"
Flying Fish FF-386
Used by permission

Though it has a kind of "country" or "ragtime" feel, Indiscretion Stomp is actually nothing more than a speeded up 12 bar blues in the key of Bb (use an Eb harp.)
The recurrent riff throughout is as follows:

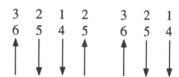

Note that the harp is employed mostly as a backup instrument during Byron Berline's expert fiddle solos and Kenny's guitar breaks. It is only in the third instrumental section that the harp really emerges for 2 solo verses, and here's what it's doing note by note:

1929 recording of George "Bullet" Williams, reputedly high on a bottle of shoe polish, playing harmonica through his nose.

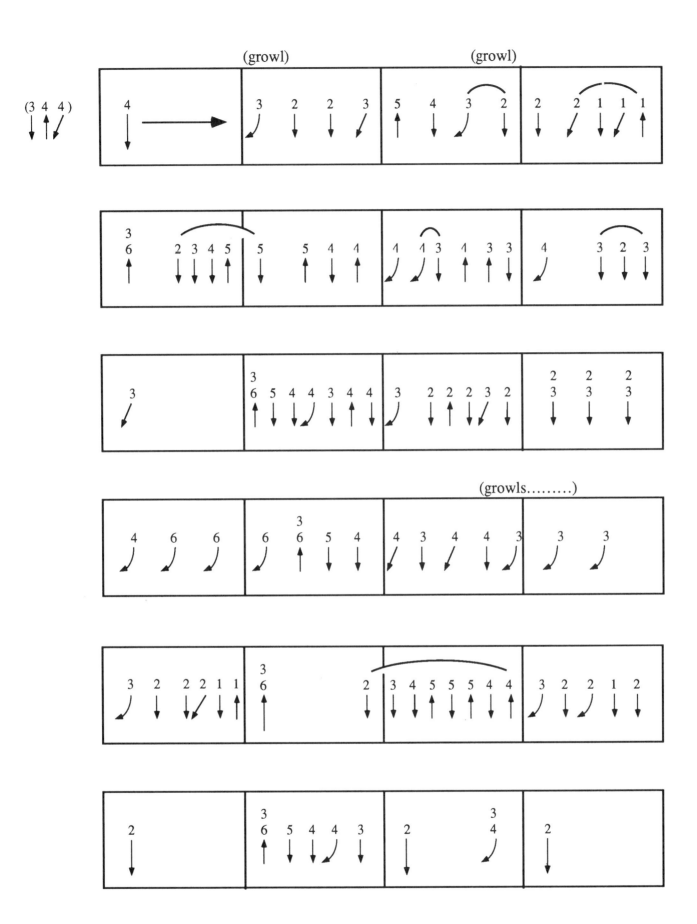

There's some very quick playing on this tune; some notes are sounded almost more by innuendo than by reality, and many bleed over the measure lines. As such, its not a solo that's easily translatable to tablature, but I think I've got it all in the above tab.

Again, notice that this is about 90% inhale, and features some of the techniques illustrated earlier (growls and octave splits.) Good luck.

YOUR MIND IS IN THE GUTTER

By Tom Ball and Kenny Sultan
Dixie Highway Music, BMI

From"Too Much Fun,"
Flying Fish FF-532
used by permission.

"Gutter" is a slow 12 bar blues in the key of A (use a D harp.) It differs from the standard 12 bar progression, however, in that most of the verses start off on the IV chord (subdominant.)

There's a funny recurrent lick that's played in unison with the guitar many times throughout this song. It employs octave splits, and goes this way:

The first solo section is Kenny's, the second is harp. Here's the note by note breakdown of the harp solo:

Sears catalog ad (courtesy Scott Dirks)

Willie Mae (Big Mama) Thornton,
Manchester, 1965

Photo by Brian Smith

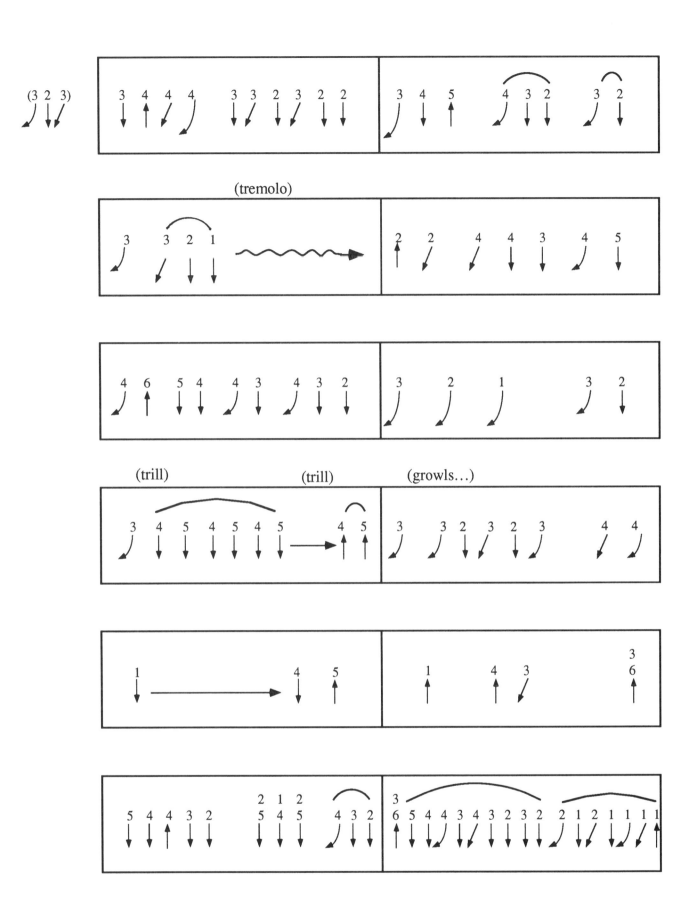

(tremolo)

(trill)　　　(trill)　　　(growls...)

Obviously the last bar is mighty tricky - on the tape it contains many partially sounded notes. This is the main crux of it, though. Remember that with the exception of the first chord, the entire last bar is inhaled, so you don't even have to think about breathing ... just take one long sustained inward breath, then slur the bent and unbent notes together, running up and down between holes 1 through 5.

EARLY
BLUES HARP ON RECORD

1877: enter Thomas Alva Edison. One day while trying to invent the telegraph, Edison accidentally discovers sound recording. He has only a distant interest in his new invention, recommending it for use as a type of dictaphone. As time passes, he barely tolerates what he perceives as it's "exploitation" as an entertainment medium. But Edison has misread the public, and almost immediately the record industry is born.

For the first 40 years, the record companies were content to release recordings by music-hall entertainers, actors, politicians and opera stars. Gramophones were an expensive novelty, and few could afford such luxury.

By 1920, however, the technology was changing: lateral-cut discs replaced Edison's cylinders, and prices became a little more realistic. Suddenly a new market was emerging, and with it, a demand for other styles of music. Soon the record companies would respond by issuing jazz, blues, country and ethnic releases to an ever-growing consumer base.

The first blues record appeared in July of 1920: <u>You Can't Keep a Good Man Down</u> by Mamie Smith (Okeh 4113.) Sales were unexpectedly high, and for the next few years, record companies rushed to release similar discs. Sadly, they were all too similar, for in attempting to cash in on the new music, producers flooded the market with dozens of virtually identical releases. The formula nearly always consisted of a contralto female singer backed by a popular swing/jazz orchestra. But the formula worked, and truly great singers like Bessie Smith, Ma Rainey, Ida Cox, and Rosa Henderson enjoyed unprecedented success.

In early 1924, the Gennett Record Company went out on a limb by breaking this pattern and releasing a rural blues performance. Thus, the first blues harmonica record was issued: Daddy Stovepipe's <u>Sundown Blues</u>. This was followed six days later by <u>Them Pitiful Blues</u>, done by a different harmonicist who called himself Stovepipe #1. Within a year or two the floodgates would open and a plethora of rural blues would emerge.

Among the top harp players recorded in the '20s and '30s were Jaybird Coleman, George "Bullet" Williams, Robert Cooksey, Chuck Darling, Blues Birdhead, Jazz Gillum, Noah Lewis, Will Shade, Jed Davenport, DeFord Bailey, El Watson, Hammie Nixon, and (amazingly) 10-year-old Walter Horton (on two 1927 sides by the Memphis Jug Band.) Horton, of course, would go on to become one of the most influential of all the postwar Chicago-style players.

In today's ultra-sophisticated world of digital technology, there is a tendency of some harmonica students to dismiss these older artists and their recordings as "rudimentary." This would be a great mistake, for these were the people planting the seeds that would reach fruition in the golden era of the mid-50s Chicago sound.

Folk Mote Music Store, Santa Barbara, CA

FIVE GREAT BLUES HARPISTS

SONNY TERRY

Sonny Terry was the undisputed king of the country blues harmonica. Born into a sharecropping family in Georgia in 1911, Sonny began to play harp at the age of 8. Two separate childhood accidents robbed him of his sight, and at that point he began to take his music more seriously; economic opportunities for those in his situation were few.

As a young man he took off for North Carolina, playing fish fries, local dances and the streets. The most lucrative locations were in front of the numerous tobacco warehouses, where men congregated before and after work-and it was in front of one of these ware-houses, in Wadesboro, that he met the great blues guitarist Blind Boy Fuller.

"Fuller was a pretty good nice guy," Sonny told Kent Cooper in *The Harp Styles of Sonny Terry*. "He'd get evil sometime but he was all right to me." Fuller was already established as a recording artist, and through him Sonny was able to travel to New York and establish himself in the studio. Their partnership ended prematurely in 1940, though, when Fuller died of kidney failure.

And so, in 1940 there began what was to be perhaps the longest musical partnership in blues history: that of the fine Knoxville guitarist Brownie McGhee and Sonny Terry. For over 40 years they played together, recording dozens of albums and touring the world. Although Sonny passed away in 1986, their recorded legacy endures, and it is a legacy rich with harmonica virtuosity.

Almost any recording featuring Sonny is recommended, but keep a special eye out for his earliest stuff - it is steeped in the rural tradition and unique in the world of blues.

SONNYBOY WILLIAMSON I

John Lee "Sonnyboy" Williamson came out of Tennessee, and has been called the father of the modern blues harp style. His recording career began the same year as Terry's (1937) but Williamson's life was cut tragically short when he was murdered with an icepick in 1948 while walking home from a gig in Chicago.

His style was something of a transitional one - a bridge between earlier rural styles and what was to come. He was an enormously influential force, especially considering he only lived to be 34 years old. Jim O'Neal is quoted in *Downbeat* as saying he was "The man who, more than anyone else, shaped the course of Chicago's classic blues of the '40s and '50s and brought the harmonica into prominence as a major blues instrument."

SONNYBOY WILLIAMSON II

Born Aleck "Rice" Miller, this "Sonnyboy" was actually older than Sonnyboy I but didn't begin his recording career until after the latter died. Implausibly, Miller claimed to be the "Original Sonnyboy Williamson. There ain't no other!"

His style was much different than that of Williamson - sparse, trembling and impeccably soulful. Miller's first recordings, for Trumpet Records in 1951, are miniature works of art - masterpieces of showmanship and austerity.

He later moved to Chicago, entering into a long and lucrative arrangement with Chess Records. A mischievous and witty man, Sonnyboy was among the first blues artists to tour extensively in Europe, and won legions of fans abroad. Sonnyboy II passed away in 1965.

LITTLE WALTER

Marion Walter Jacobs is considered by many blues players to have been the greatest of them all. Certainly there can be no disputing his tremendously influential sound - a sound still highly imitated today.

Walter was born in Louisiana in 1930, but ran away from home at the age of 12. Throughout his teenage years he lived on the streets, playing for tips and scuffling. Eventually he worked his way up to Chicago, where he made his first record (for Ora Nelle) at the age of 17, then fell into the Muddy Waters band.

In 1952, at the end of a recording session, Walter went into an impromptu instrumental. Leonard Chess apparently liked what he heard, and issued the untitled work as "Juke" by "Little Walter and his Night Cats." It became number 1 on the R & B charts, and redefined the role of harmonica in the blues context.

Ironically, the song did so well that Walter left Muddy's band and hit the road on his own, replaced by Junior Wells. And although he continued to record with Muddy until 1958, Little Walter never again toured with Muddy Waters.

Despite a series of brilliant recordings, Jacobs never quite retained his earlier popularity. His personality was difficult and he seemed to distrust promoters and even fellow musicians almost to the point of paranoia. As his self-destructive habits escalated, he became notoriously unreliable and unhappy, and in 1968, died as a result of injuries sustained in a fight. He was 37 years old.

For all his faults, Walter's preeminence in his field cannot be questioned. Virtually everything he recorded was masterful, and his contributions are incalculable. To most players, Little Walter is The Man.

BIG WALTER

If Little Walter had the chops, Big Walter had the tone! Walter Horton was born in Mississippi and picked up harp at the age of 5, making his recording debut in 1927 at the ripe old age of 10 (with the Memphis Jug Band; "Sometimes I Think I Love You," and "Sunshine Blues.") He worked as a child with the Memphis Jug Band in the Ma Rainey Show, and with Honeyboy Edwards, then moved to Memphis when his father got a job with the city.

By 1951 he was recording for Sam Phillips, and a series of beautiful records emerged for labels like Modern, Sun, States, Cobra and J.O.B. For a time, he too played with Muddy Waters until he was fired for "unreliability."

Horton was an unusual man, quirky and unpredictable. He called everyone, regardless of gender or age, "Grampa." When I first met Walter in 1966, I recall asking him if he still played "Hard Hearted Woman,"' a harmonica tour-de-force he had recorded in the '50s. Walter vehemently denied ever having recorded (or even having heard of) the song, and became visibly angry and upset about it. An hour later he played a masterful, 15-minute version.

Willie Dixon, in his autobiography *I Am The Blues* said of Big Walter: "You couldn't whistle, sing, hum or play a rhythm of anything that he couldn't do like you wanted ... he'd take a beer can, cut the top out of it, cup the harmonica in there and make that sonuvagun sound like a trombone and no one could tell the difference."

Big Walter was a genius at vibrato and dynamics, and his playing ranks among the most eloquent of all. He passed away in 1981.

"MELODY KING." Hotz Harmonica. Double sided, tremolo in 2 different keys, 64 reeds, 5 inches long.
No. 084 ....**$0.75**

"CHROMATIC." Koch Harmonica. A simple push of the lever operates the half tones easily. (Sharps and flats). 40 reeds, 5¼ inches long.
No. 980 ....**$2.00**

Little Willie Anderson
Billy Boy Arnold
Steve Baker
Carey Bell
Billy Bizor
Sonny Blair
Juke Boy Bonner
Billy Branch
Grace Brim
Buster Brown
Norton Buffalo
George Buford
Dave Burgin
Eddie Burns
J. C. Burris
Wild Child Butler
Paul Butterfield
Eddie Clarke
William Clarke
Henry Clement
Schoolboy Cleve
Willie Cobbs
Sonny Cooper
James Cotton
James Dalton
Paul DeLay
Bill Dicey
Bob Dylan
Rick Epping
Rick Estrin
Harmonica Frank Floyd
Mark Ford
Forest City Joe
Little Willie Foster
Frank Frost
Jesse Fuller
P. T. Gazell
Pete Glaser
Tony Glover
Good Rockin' Charles

John Hammond
James Harman
Harmonica Fats
Harmonica Slim
Slim Harpo
John Lee Henley
Salty Holmes
Mark Hummel
Andy Irvine
Zaven Jambasian
Mitch Kashmar
Walter Liniger
Lazy Lester
Howard Levy
Huey Lewis
Papa Lightfoot
Juke Logan
Joe Hill Louis
Hot Shot Love
Robert Lucas
Mel Lyman
Lee McBee
Jerry McCain
Charlie McCoy
Robert Lee McCoy
David McKelvey
Rory McLeod
Magic Dick
Taj Mahal
Sidney Maiden
Johnny Mars
John Mayall
George Mayweather
Elmon Mickle
Charlie Musselwhite
Louis Myers
Sammy Myers
Kenny Neal
Raful Neal
Paul Oscher

Lee Oskar
Fred Palmer
Junior Parker
Peg Leg Sam
Rod Piazza
Gary Primich
Jerry Portnoy
Snooky Pryor
Mickey Raphael
Jimmy Reed
Robert Richard
Dr. Isiah Ross
Peter Madcat Ruth
Curtis Salgado
Will Scarlet
John Sebastian
Shakey Jake
Corky Siegel
Little Mack Simmons
Chris Smith
George Smith
Whispering Smith
Stormy Herman
Henry Strong
Sugar Blue
Fingers Taylor
Toots Thielmans
Kid Thomas
Big Mama Thornton
James Walton
Jordan Webb
Glenn Weiser
Junior Wells
Mark Wenner
Phil Wiggins
Alan Wilson
Kim Wilson
Howlin' Wolf
Stevie Wonder
John Wrencher

And these are just the ones I know about! It seems like new great harp blowers are surfacing every week, so if I inadvertently omitted you or your favorite, my apologies. (Write your own book, sorehead!)

RECOMMENDED RECORDINGS

At the risk of sounding repetitive, I recommend that for every hour spent practicing, spend at least 2 hours listening! It will be extremely difficult (if not impossible) to get any good on harp without thoroughly immersing yourself in the sound - and you may as well listen to the best.

Here are some of the greatest blues harmonica recordings. At the time this goes to press (1993,) most of these are available on CD, some only on LP. As the technology changes, a lot of the LP-only recordings will no doubt surface on CD, and the release numbers may change as a result. When possible, I've listed the CD numbers.
Items considered essential are marked with an asterisk (*)

SONNY TERRY
* Sonny Terry 1938-1955 Document DLP 536
* The Folkways Years (1944-1963) Folkways SF 40033
  Whoopin' The Blues Charly 1120
  Sonny's Story Fantasy OBC 503
* Sonny Is King! Fantasy OBC 521
  California Blues Fantasy FCD 24723-2
  Whoopin' Alligator 4734

SONNYBOY WILLIAMSON I
  Volume 1 Blues Classics 3
* Volume 2 Blues Classics 20
  Volume 3 Blues Classics 24

SONNYBOY WILLIAMSON II
* King Biscuit Time Arhoolie 310
  Goin' In Your Direction Trumpet AA-801
  One Way Out MCA CHD 9116
  Down And Out Blues MCA CHD 31272
  Real Folk Blues MCA CHD 9272
  More Real Folk Blues MCA CHD 9277
  Bummer Road MCA CHD 9324
  Keep It To Ourselves Alligator 4787

LITTLE WALTER
* The Best of Little Walter MCA CHD 9192
* The Best of Little Walter volume 2 MCA, CHD 9292
* Boss Blues Harmonica MCA CHD 92503
* Hate To See You Go MCA CHD 9321
  The Blues World of Delmark 648
  Blue and Lonesome Le Roi du Blues 33.2007
  Southern Feeling Le Roi du Blues 33.2012

WALTER HORTON
* Fine Cuts Blind Pig 0678
  Can't Keep Lovin' You Blind Pig 1484
  Harmonica Blues Kings Pearl 12
  Little Boy Blue JSP CD 208
* The Soul of Blues Harmonica Argo (out of print)

Racist Diatribe, c 1950's

MUDDY WATERS
* The Chess Box MCA CHD 3-80002
* The Best Of Muddy Waters MCA CHD 31268
  Rare and Unissued MCA CHD 9180
  Real Folk Blues MCA CHD 9274
  More Real Folk Blues MCA CHD 9278

JUNIOR WELLS
* Hoodoo Man Blues Delmark
  612 Southside Blues Delmark 628
  On Tap Delmark 635
* Blues Hit Big Town Delmark 640

JAMES COTTON
  High Compression Alligator 4737
  Live Alligator 4746
  Take Me Back Blind Pig 2587

HOWLIN' WOLF
  Cadillac Daddy Rounder SS28
  Change My Way MCA CHD 93001
* The Chess Box MCA CHD 9332
  Moanin' In The Moonlight MCA CHD 5908
  Real Folk Blues MCA CHD 9279
  More Real Folk Blues MCA CHD 9273

OTHER HARPISTS
  Norton Buffalo & Roy Rogers, R&B, Blind Pig 4491
  John Cephas & Phil Wiggins, Dog Days of August, Flying Fish 394
  John Cephas & Phil Wiggins, Guitar Man, Flying Fish 470
  William Clarke, BIowin' Like Hell, Alligator 4788
  Fabulous Thunderbirds (Kim Wilson),Girls Go Wild, Chrysalis 1250
  Frank Frost, Jellyroll King, Charly 223
  Jazz Gillum, Roll Dem Bones, Wolf WBJCD 002
  John Hammond, Nobody But You, Flying Fish 502
  John Hammond, Live!, Rounder 3074
  James Harman, Extra Napkins, Rivera 505
  James Harman, Do Not Disturb, Blacktop 1065
* Slim Harpo, The Best Of Rhino 106
  Lazy Lester, Harp and Soul, Alligator 4768
* Memphis Jug Band (Will Shade) Yazoo 1067
  Charlie Musselwhite, Ace Of Harps, Alligator 4781
  Charlie Musselwhite, Signature, Alligator 4801
  Sam Myers w/ Anson Funderburgh, Sins, Blacktop 1038
  Rod Piazza, Blues in the Dark, Blacktop 1062
  Pontiax (Mitch Kashmar), 100 Miles to Go, Spitfire 017
  Snooky Pryor, Snooky, Blind Pig 2387
  Snooky Pryor, Back to the Country, Blind Pig 4391
* Jimmy Reed, 18 Greatest Hits, Motown 9065
  Jimmy Reed, Big Boss Blues, Charly 3
  Jimmy Reed, Ride 'Em On Down, Charly 171
* Dr. Ross, Call The Doctor, Testament 2206
* George Smith, Oopin' Doopin' Doopin', Ace CH 60
  Big Mama Thornton, Ball and Chain, Arhoolie 305

The <u>Yerba</u> <u>Buena</u> <u>Blues</u> band at the Easter Sunday Love-in,
Elysian Park, 1967

CLOCK-WISE FROM TOP LEFT;
Tom Ball; Bret Lopez, John Koenig,
Frank Hardman; Bret Lopez;
Tom Ball.

Photo's by Pete Armstrong

Also, if you should have any questions regarding this book, or would like any info about our recordings, or just want to say "hi," feel free to write me at:

Tom Ball - P.O. Box 20156 - Santa Barbara, CA., 93120

Incidentally, I should mention that if you're interested in blues guitar, Kenny has some very fine books available, also with Centerstream Publishing. (I figure if I plug his books, he'll hafta plug mine!)

Good luck with your playing, and let me hear from you,

Yours in blues,

Tom Ball

PS - I am still seeking to complete my collection of Sonny Terry 78s. If you should have any for sale or trade, please drop me a note.

"BLUE RIBBON." Hotz Harmonica. 10 single holes, 20 reeds, 4 inches long.

No. 00 .... **$0.25**

"AMERICAN ACE." Hotz Harmonica. 10 single holes, 20 reeds, 4 inches long.

No. 02 .... **$0.30**

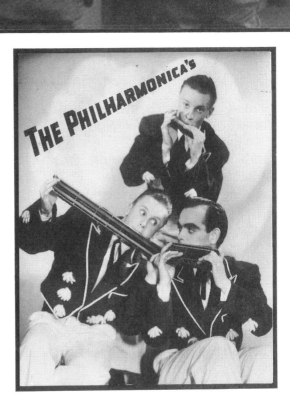

Muddy Waters

65

THE EVOLUTION OF A HARP BLOWER

Well, the publishers asked me to wind this up with a few pages on my own musical history, so please bear with me. Here goes:

My folks grew up in Santa Monica, CA., and I came along in 1950, on Sonny Terry's birthday, October 24. My father, James, had played drums in his teens, but family considerations precluded any thoughts of his pursuing it as a career.

The family was always interested in music, but I can't say that we played a lot of it around the house, except on the record player. For awhile my father had a set of vibes with which he drove us all crazy, and we had an old upright piano that nobody played. My mother, Lolita, has always directed her creative energies towards the arts and crafts.

When I was 10 or 11 the folks gave me a guitar for Christmas, a small Japanese nylon-string called an Orpheus. It wasn't bad; very sturdy -the kind of guitar you could drop off the roof or use for a baseball bat. With the guitar came a few lessons with a young man named Dave Zeitlin who set me off on the right path, steering me away from surf music and towards Woody Guthrie, Leadbelly and Lightnin' Hopkins. He also told me about the various radio shows where I could hear this kind of stuff, and about the Ash Grove, a club which was later to be one of the most important factors in my musical education.

"... and a blues harp. And please bring yourself a breath mint. .." 1954

Bob Dylan's early records were surfacing just then, so for a year or two I zoomed around on my skateboard trying to be a prepubescent junior Dylan, with a homemade harp rack and an F. R. Hotz harmonica. My friend Pat Pierce showed me a couple licks on harp. Then one day I heard Brownie McGhee and Sonny Terry on the radio.

Sonny's playing blew me away! It was so much more complex and interesting than anything I'd heard before. This led to several years of immersing myself in the world of blues, buying, borrowing, taping and studying every recording I could get my hands on. Soon I had the blues because I didn't have the blues.

About this time, my older brother Steve got himself a five-string banjo and began learning Scruggs-style picking. After awhile he got pretty good at it, and this opened up another new realm: bluegrass. At first I couldn't stand the stuff; it took some time, but I grew to love the high lonesome sound.

At about 14 I discovered the Ash Grove, a small blues and folk club that used to be on Melrose in Hollywood. The first night I went there they had Mance Lipscomb and Lightnin' Hopkins - I was hooked. Of course, I should've realized even back then that you couldn't get rich from that kind of music: there were about 30 people in the audience, and admission was $2.

With another pickin' pal named Ryan Richelson, I became an Ash Grove habitue. Over the next 5 or 6 years I spent as many nights there as possible, meeting, talking to, listening to and even sitting in with many of my musical heroes. I can only express awe at the tolerance of these musicians for putting up with us little punks hanging out and bugging them with innumerable dumb questions.

At about 15 I became good friends with 3 high-school contemporaries who were already accomplished guitarists: Carl Buffa, John Koenig and Bret Lopez. These guys showed me how to fingerpick, and hipped me to Blind Blake and Joseph Spence.

Bret and John had just formed a band, and somehow I got asked to be in it as a singer and harp blower. The band was called the Yerba Buena Blues Band, and it held together for a couple of years.

Although we pretty much stunk it up, (especially me,) the Yerba Buena managed to play many of the top Sunset Strip and Hollywood clubs like the Sea Witch, Mother Neptune's and P.J.'s. *Aspirin Magazine* called us "the band most likely to blow their own minds at Armageddon," whatever the hell that meant. The biggest gig we did was the Easter Sunday 1967 Love-In at Elysian Park, an event the *L.A. Times* called "the Easter Sunday Freak Out...a rejoicing of the rejected." I was 16 years old and scared to death, playing for 10,000 people on a bill with the Turtles, the Peanut Butter Conspiracy, Chambers Brothers, Boz Scaggs, Hoyt Axton, some of the biggest names of the '60s. I needn't have worried, though, since much of the crowd seemed to be in some sort of an altered state. Musta been all that incense.

In '67 we did 3 recording sessions for the Good Time Jazz label. None of it was released, but the experience was invaluable. After high school the Yerba Buena broke up, and for the next 10 years or so I was musically inactive, at least on a professional level.

Like a lot of '60s young folks, I spent much of the next decade abroad, bumming around the world and soaking up musical influences. I paused long enough to get married and divorced, a brief union that resulted in my lovely daughter Shannon, who is now grown and a professional singer working the cruise-ship circuit.

In the late '70s, my girlfriend Laurie (now my wife) and I moved up to Santa Barbara. Soon I made the acquaintance of my future partner Kenny Sultan, and the rest, as they say, is history. Since 1979, Kenny and I have managed to record 5 albums and tour the world a few times, so I guess I can't complain too much.

We're still based out of Santa Barbara, and I don't envision that changing for awhile, so if you ever find yourself out this way, feel free to drop Kenny or me a note; we'll let you know where we're gigging. Unless we're out on a tour, we play the California central coast fairly regularly.

Tom and Kenny, Gaildorfer Blues Festival, Germany 1991

ANTHOLOGIES

*   Harmonica Blues of the 20s and 30s, Yazoo 1053
*   Great Harmonica Players, Roots RL 321
        Harmonica Showcase 1927-1931, Matchbox 218
        Harmonica Blues 1936-1940, Wolf 109
*   Chicago Blues - the Early 50s, Blues Classics 8
        Sun Records Harmonica Classics, Rounder SS 29
        Lowdown Memphis Harmonica Jam 1950-1955, Nighthawk 103
        Chicago Slickers1948-1953, Nighthawk 102
        Chicago Slickers vol. 2, Nighthawk107
        Memphis Blues, United//Superior7779
        Low Blows, Rooster 7610
        Harp Attack, Alligator 4790
        Blow By Blow, Sundown 709 01
        Suckin' and Blowin', Sundown 709 03
        Juicy Harmonica, Sundown 709 06

VIDEOTAPE

*   Reverend Gary Davis and Sonny Terry ,Yazoo 501

Howlin' Wolf

TOM BALL AND KENNY SULTAN DISCOGRAPHY
(WITH HARP KEYS)

One of the biggest problems beginners have in playing along with records can be the actual determination of the harp key.

Over the last decade or so, I've been asked many times by harpists who want to play along, what key a given song is in, particularly songs from our records. Below is a list of all the guitar and harmonica songs Kenny and I have recorded, also the song key (followed by the key of the harp used.)

"Confusion" Sonyatone Records # ST-1006 Released 1981, out of print
Confusion E,(A)
Tater Pie F,(Bb)
Greyhound Blues F,(Bb)
Five Long Years C,(F)
My Gal C, (F)
Changed The Lock E,(A)
Outskirts of Town F,(Bb)
Can't Remember E,(A)

"Who Drank My Beer" Kicking Mule Records #KM-176 Released 1983, out of print
Who Drank My Beer E,(A)
He's In The Jailhouse Now C,(F)
When the Judge Pounds the Gavel F,(Bb)
One Monkey Don't Stop the Show G,(C)
One Eyed San G,(C)
Television C,(F)
V-8 Ford F#,(B)
Solid Gone E,(A)
Bail Out E,(A)
Fishin' Blues G,(C)

"Bloodshot Eyes" Flying Fish Records #FF-386 Released 1986, Available all 3 formats
Too Many Drivers E,(A & high-A)
Bloodshot Eyes, A, (D)
Long Distance Call F,(Bb)
Street Walkin' Woman A,(D)
Your Red Wagon E/F,(A,Bb)
Indiscretion Stomp Bb,(Eb)
Don't Burn The Candle at Both Ends F,(Bb)
That'll Never Happen No More A,(D)
Fool About a Cigarette E,(A)

"Too Much Fun" Flying Fish Records #FF-532 Released 1990 , All 3 formats
Too Much Fun E,(A)
My Gal C,(G)
Chicken Ala Blues F,(Bb)
Long Legged Woman A,(D)
It Should've Been Me F,(Bb)
How Can I Miss You When You Won't Go Away Eb,(Ab)
Your Mind Is In The Gutter A,(D)
Fly Hen Blues G,(C)
Days Like This E, (A)
A Dollar Down G, (C)

"Filthy Rich"
Flying Fish Records #619 Released in 1993, Available in Cass. & CD
My Six Reasons D, (high G)
My Last Meal F, (Bb)
Don't Pay Me No Mind E, (A)
Whiskey Bent and Hell Bound F#, (B)
All Talk and No Action E, (A)
Filthy Rich G, (C)
Honey Bee E, (A)
Mind Your Own Business E, (A)
Cigarette Blues Eb, (Ab)
Tater Pie F, (Bb & low F)
When the Evenin' Sun Goes Down G, (C)

"Double Vision"
Flying Fish/Rounder Records #656. Released in 1996. CD only
Perfect Woman C, (F)
Your Shoes Don't Fit Feet E, (A)
No Money, No Honey E, (A)
Automobile Mechanic G, (C)
I Feel Alright Now B, (E)
Sweet Temptation A, (D)
Sloppy Joe Db, (Ab)
Television C, (F)
Roll Of The Tumblin' Dice E, (A)
Ride That Train E, (A)
Back To California B, (E)
Who Drank My Beer? E, (A)

"Tom Ball & Kenny Sultan 20th Anniversary LIVE!"
No Guru Entertainment, Inc. # 2000-2 Released in 2000. CD only
Your Red Wagon E/F, (A/Bb)
Filthy Rich G, (C)
Honey Bee E, (A)
He's In The Jailhouse Now C, (F)
All Talk And No Action E, (A)
Dallas Rag/Harlem Rag
One Monkey Don't Stop The Show F#, (B)
Nightcrawler B, (E)
Fishin' Blues G, (C)
Berceuse: Cancion de Cuna
Automobile Mechanic G, (C)
Tired As A Man Can Be E, (A)
You Can't Stop Father Time G, (C)
It Should've Been Me F, (Bb)
Kidney Stew F, (Bb)
Perfect Woman C, (F)

Recorded Live In Concert at Victoria Hall, Santa Barbara, California

PSEUDONYMS OF BLUES HARMONICISTS

At some point a lot of fans and players of blues harmonica start to get involved in collecting old records, a pursuit which can be both frustrating and amusing due to pseudonyms.

A look through the blues discographies can reveal an amazing level of creativity: artists with names like Daddy Hotcakes, Peanut the Kidnapper, Sweet Papa Tadpole, Ironing Board Sam and hundreds more.

The reasons for pseudonymous releases were varied, but one good reason was economic. Often, blues artists were tied up under exclusive contract to one label, and may or may not have been paid royalties. In order to survive, some would simultaneously record for competing labels using an alias. Many of the blues labels were aware of this practice, and were fairly tolerant of it. By way of example, the great John Lee Hooker made 78s as John Lee Booker, John Lee Cooker, John L. Hooker, John L. Booker, John Lee, Johnny Lee, Johnny Williams, Delta John, Texas Slim, The Boogie Man, Birmingham Sam, and Sir John Lee Hooker.

The following is a list of aliases under which prominent blues harpists recorded, in rough chronological order from the mid 1920s to the early 1960s. Happy Hunting!

Daddy Stovepipe is Johnny Watson
Sunny Jim is Johnny Watson
Stovepipe # I Jim is Sam Jones
Rabbit's Foot Williams is Jaybird Coleman
Harmonica Tim is James Simons
Blues Birdhead is James Simons
The Carolina Peanut Boys are Noah Lewis' band
Bill McKinley is Jazz Gillum
Sanders Terry is Sonny Terry
Sonnyboy Williamson (on Bluebird and Victor) is John Lee Williamson (Sonnyboy #1)
Sonnyboy Williamson (on Trumpet, Ace, Checker, Chess) is Rice Miller (Sonnyboy #2)
Sonny Boy Williams (on Decca) is Enoch Williams, (who is not a harp player)
Sonny Williams (on Super Disc) is Enoch Williams, (not a harp player)
Sonnyboy Williamson (on Ram) is none of the above, an unknown different harp player
Sunnyboy and his Pals (on Gennett) is Papa Harvey Hull, (not a harp player)
Chicago Sunny Boy is Joe Hill Louis
Johnny Lewis is Joe Hill Louis
Little Joe is Joe Hill Louis
Little Walter is Walter Jacobs
Big Walter (on Peacock) is Walter Price, (not a harp player)
Big Walter (on States and Cobra) is Walter Horton
Mumbles is Walter Horton
Shakey Horton is Walter Horton
Driftin' Slim is Elmon Mickle
Driftin' Smith is Elmon Mickle
Harmonica Harry is Elmon Mickle
Model T Slim is Elmon Mickle
George Allen is George Smith
Harmonica King is George Smith
Little Walter Jr. is George Smith
Muddy Waters Jr. is Mojo Buford